Augustine Birrell

Four lLctures on the Law of Employers Liability at Home and

Abroad

Augustine Birrell

Four lLctures on the Law of Employers Liability at Home and Abroad

ISBN/EAN: 9783744727211

Printed in Europe, USA, Canada, Australia, Japan

Cover: Foto ©Andreas Hilbeck / pixelio.de

More available books at **www.hansebooks.com**

BY

AUGUSTINE BIRRELL, M.P.

ONE OF HER MAJESTY'S COUNSEL
AND QUAIN PROFESSOR OF LAW AT UNIVERSITY COLLEGE, LONDON

London

MACMILLAN AND CO., Limited

NEW YORK: THE MACMILLAN COMPANY

1897

RICHARD CLAY AND SONS, LIMITED,
LONDON AND BUNGAY.

PREFATORY NOTE

THESE four Lectures formed part of a longer course delivered by me during this year at Lincoln's Inn as Quain Professor of Law at University College, London. The only reason why they were delivered in Lincoln's Inn and not at University College was the convenience of the students who attended them.

A. B.

3 NEW SQUARE, LINCOLN'S INN,
    June 14, 1897.

CONTENTS

THE EMPLOYERS' LIABILITY AT COMMON LAW

IT was for a time the favourite theory of Mr. Froude that our national movement, that procession of affairs which, whether you call it "progress," or by any other name, exerts the strangest fascination over the imaginative student of history, was nowhere else so faithfully recorded as in the preambles to our Acts of Parliament. For a theory it was not a bad one, but it applies only to that time when preambles were long and enactments short. Modern Statutes, for the most part, have no preambles, our stingy legislators being averse to give the judges any clue to their meaning beyond the bare text. Nowadays, however, important legislation is usually, though by no means always, heralded by discussion both in the House of Commons and out of it; and from the nature of this discussion, and from the general object of the legislation which is its outcome, the observer may gain an insight into social conditions and relations at least as trustworthy as from those old and picturesque preambles to which Mr. Froude was so much attached.

The great interest excited by and the importance attributed to legislation affecting the liability, whether civil or criminal, of employers towards their workmen for injuries sustained by the latter in the course of their employment, mark an epoch in our history. Slowly, very slowly, the workman, the man who lives by his arms and his legs on a weekly or daily wage, has forced himself to the front, and demands of the two sources of the law, the legislator and the judge (and of the law of master and servant the greater part has sprouted from the brains of judges), that in the consideration of the terms of the Contract of Hiring, the facts of the case, as they press upon the owner of the arms and legs, shall have due prominence given them.

We were once a nation of shopkeepers, and our ideas corresponded with our vocation. We are now, so far as we have not all gone upon the Stock Exchange, a vast industrial enterprise, carried on by night as well as day, by shifts of men, and amidst "the hideous hum" of machinery. The problems that to-day demand solution, if justice is to be done between man and man, require wider views and a set of ideas which never crossed the minds of the Temple-bred judges of the last generation, who, perched on high, and usually amenable to no more searching tribunal than two of their Brethren sitting in Banco, not only interpreted with an easy mind contracts between employers and their workmen, but read into those contracts terms and provisions of which neither of the contracting parties had ever heard, and few of them even yet understand.

This interest, this almost feverish interest, is by no means confined to Great Britain. The great wave of industrialism has gone over the whole Continent of Europe; and we are accordingly well supplied with Blue Books and Foreign Office Memoranda, from which we may learn, with varying degrees of inaccuracy, what Germany and Austria have done, and what France is still talking about doing, in this matter of the arms and legs, the hands and fingers, not to say the lives of their huge working populations. Here at home the Government has, as you must have noticed, introduced into Parliament a Bill for providing workmen with compensation for accidents, which is now attracting—and well does it deserve to attract—the friendly though close and critical attention of millions of men, employers and employed, to whose business and bosoms it mightily appeals and closely relates.

This fierce light beating upon our British Themis is not only very trying to the complexion of so elderly a dame, but proves very disconcerting to her, upsetting, as it does, her traditional methods, her ancient tests, and her nicely calculated " less and mores." An eminent Chancery practitioner, afterwards a Vice-Chancellor, on being informed on one occasion that the actual suitor in a litigation wished to attend consultation, roughly forbade his doing so, saying, " I will have no flesh and blood in my chambers." No doubt flesh and blood are

very apt to disturb the mental repose of a
positive opinion, but they cannot be kept
out of either an Employers' Liability or
a Workmen's Compensation for Accidents
Bill.

Two facts of modern life have greatly
affected the question. One is machinery, and
the other is joint stock and limited liability
enterprise. Neither need detain me. Machinery is dangerous, and grows more so every
day. But last week I saw a young fellow,
twenty-five years old—a married man with
two children—both of whose hands had been
cut off by a printing machine. It was as
cleanly done as could be, but a terrible, an
afflicting spectacle. Could we collect together
on the 22nd of next June the vast army of
those who during Her Majesty's reign have
been maimed by machinery, it would be a
woeful sight and a melancholy commentary
on our methods of production. To dwell longer
on this aspect of the case would be improper,
but to forget all about it would be to leave
" Hamlet " out of the play.

As for joint stock and limited liability
companies, I will only say that in the opinion

of some critics of the Human Comedy the two most remarkable achievements of the Queen's reign are the Companies' Acts of 1862 and onwards, and the establishment of the Divorce Court in 1857.

I hastily return to my subject; and before engaging in any of its subtleties, let us have the courage to be elementary. I love the elements of all questions, even of geometry— the pure mountain stream before it has become defiled and discoloured by the garbage and poisonous effluent of rival sophisters.

In all the codes and systems of law of Western nations we find provision made for the payment of damages in respect of injury to person or to property occasioned by negligence; nor, despite the refinements of lawyers struggling to distinguish one case from another, the wholly superfluous and unpaid malignancy of metaphysicians and the tiresome pedantry of grammarians, has any one ever doubted what he meant by negligence. He means, and he has always meant, the absence of that amount of care which each man in this our social state owes his fellow. What that amount of care is in the circumstances of each particular case is

another matter. Here we get our first peep
of that woeful vista, down which we see sport-
ing in the shade eminent judges and ani-
mated counsel ; solicitors in the well ; bags,
briefs and bills ; and there may we also discern,
less obviously cheerful, the anxious suitor, the
bewildered witness, trying hard to remember
the difference between the truth and what he
had said in his proof—perjury, misery and mad-
ness ! But so long as we stick to the blessed
elements we shall not be troubled with this
crew. But there they are, all the same,
awaiting us.

As a matter of law then, both at home and
abroad, this liability of one man to another to
make good a personal injury, sustained in
consequence of an absence of a proper
amount of care, is a branch of the law of
negligence. It begins and ends in negligence,
in a breach of duty—of the legal duty
I owe my neighbour not to hurt him. If I
meant him harm, if I wittingly lured him or
cruelly abandoned him to a fate I had pre-
pared for him, I am not careless but criminal ;
but if, wishing him no evil—nay, though over-
flowing with amiable sentiments towards him

—I yet do or omit to do something (which I
ought not to have done)or which I should have
done, and in consequence of my act or omission harm befalls him, I must pay what a jury
finds or agreement determines to be his due,
either in full, or such a dividend in the pound as
in the event of my bankruptcy may be offici-
ally declared.

Here then you perceive, staring you in the
face, on the very threshold of the subject, the
difference between the law of negligence and
the law of insurance or warranty against accident. The law very easily might have been
that every man warranted to the full extent of
his pecuniary capacity that never would he, in
any circumstances, occasion hurt to his neighbour. But this is not the law, either at home
or abroad.

First example.—Driving my gig furiously,
or, as I should probably be forced to admit,
" at a smartish pace," down the High Street I
run over a chimney-sweep, who in a sober
fashion is crossing the road. He is in the
hospital for six weeks. Clearly I must pay.
I owed him a duty so to drive my gig as not
to injure him. I failed in my duty and must

pay ; and this by the common law of England, the birthright of every subject.

This example covers a great number of other cases occurring in what Wordsworth has feelingly called "the dreary intercourse of daily life."

Second example.—Instead of driving the gig myself, I being laudably anxious to fulfil my duty to my neighbour and to love him as myself and thus avoid all risk of paying damages, employ a coachman who came to me highly recommended by a timid old lady, in whose service he had been as coachman for ten years without a fault being discovered in him. On engaging him I gave him the strictest orders never to drive quickly down the High Street, orders which he always obeyed until the hapless morn when he ran over a chimney-sweep. He is, of course, liable—but then, so am I. Now why? What harm have I done? What could I have done more than I did? What duty to my sooty friend have I broken? Negligence, we know, is such a lack of care as in the circumstances amounts to a breach of duty. A person in my employment who is fully competent to discharge the particular

duty I entrust to him does something in de-
fiance of my authority and contrary to my
expressed wishes which injures somebody.
How am I negligent? Why should I pay?

The aid of Latin is, of course, invoked.
When in difficulties quote Latin. *Respondeat
superior*, it is said. But why should he?
That is the whole question. Nothing is gained
by repeating a proposition which has been
challenged in another tongue. *Respondeat
superior* is the formula imposing the liability,
not a reason for the imposition. Driven out
of this cover, refuge is sought in the maxim,
Qui facit per alium, facit per se; but this
maxim simply reeks of agency, and agency is
based upon authority, which may be either
particular or general, either express or implied.
Thus, if I authorise a house agent to sell my
house for £5,000, and he sells it for that
figure, I am bound *qui facit per alium, facit
per se;* but if he purports to let it go as a
great bargain for £3,000, I am not bound, for
I have done nothing *per alium.* It was the
alius who has tried to do something *per me.*
This is the case of particular authority. If a
man by his conduct holds out another as his

general agent, by permitting him to act in that character and deal with the world as a general agent, he must be taken to be the general agent for the person who so allows him to act, and the principal is bound, even though in the particular instance the agent may have exceeded his authority. This no doubt goes a long way, but it is all based upon authority, express or implied, to do the act in question. But who will say that a coachman driving furiously down a street, contrary to his master's orders, has implied authority to run over a chimney-sweep?

The only ground for this enormous extension of the law of negligence which covers all the cases of injuries done to the outside public by servants acting within the scope of their proper employment, though in the course of it flatly disobeying their master's orders, is this :—If a man chooses to carry on the operations of his life and business by hiring others to do the work for him, he can only be allowed to do so on the terms of guaranteeing the capacity of his servants to answer for acts and defaults committed by them in the course of the work he has ordered them to do. (*See* judgment of Blackburn, J., in *Williams* v. *Jones*, 3 H. and C. 609.)

But, of course, the real pinch of the case, and the social necessity for the rule, was to find somebody to pay the chimney-sweep what justice declared to be his due. Were coachmen always what they only sometimes are, men of fortune and able to pay for the luxury of running over an occasional foot-passenger, the sweep would have been content with his remedy against the actual wrong-doer; but usually the owner of the gig is the more responsible of the two, and therefore somehow or another he must be made to pay.

Here, then, we get our first glimpse of the logician and the moralist being shoved rudely on one side in order to find somebody to make it up to the chimney-sweep.

This law—*Respondeat superior*—is, I need hardly add, judge-made. It does not appear to be of great antiquity, for, in the *Year Book*, 9 Henry VI. 53 B, it is laid down (I am indebted to Mr. Bevan for the reference), "If a servant whose duty it is to sell merchandise sells an unsound horse or other merchandise in a fair, no action lies against the master for deceit, since he did not sell to any person in particular." But cases do soon begin to make their appearance, going to show that masters were liable at common law for their servants' misdeeds; and, in the famous case of *Turberville* v. *Stampe*, decided in 1697, reported 1 *Lord Raymond*, 264, it was authoritatively determined by Lord Holt that a master is responsible for his servant's torts.

The common law of England, therefore, stands thus :—*First*, a master is liable for his own negligence, both to his own workmen and to the general public, assuming, in the case of a member of the public, that he had some right to be where he was when he sustained the personal injury he complains of; and, *Secondly*, a master is liable, according to the formula *Respondeat superior*, for damage sustained by any one by reason of the negligence of any of the master's servants acting within the scope of their proper employment, subject to the limitation first made known in 1837 by the case of *Priestley* v. *Fowler*.

Leaving this case out of mind for the moment, the common law covered the whole ground, and upon it certain questions necessarily arose, still arise, and always must arise, if matters of the kind are to be judicially investigated and determined according to this law. The questions are—Who is a master? Who is a servant? Was the servant acting within the scope of his employment? Was the injury occasioned by the negligence of the master or his servant?

These questions are, I repeat, inevitable; but our common law proceeds to put two further questions, not quite so inevitable, yet far from irrelevant. The first of these additional questions is, Was the negligence (and here I assume the fact of the negligence has been found) the proximate cause of the accident? for if it was not, then the causal connection between the negligence of the master or servant, and the accident which has occurred is severed. What, one instantly asks, can sever this causal connection in actual practice? and the answer is, the injured man's own negligence, or, to employ ominous words, sounding in costs, his contributory negligence. Lord Bowen, in *Thomas* v. *Quartermaine*, 18 Q. B. D. 694, has defined contributory negligence as meaning " that the plaintiff has himself contributed to the accident in such a sense as to render the defendant's breach of duty no longer its proximate cause."

This, you will see, assumes that the employer (if it be a case of master and servant) ought only to pay if his breach of duty be the proximate cause of the accident, which is often a very nice inquiry, upon which judges have differed with great frequency. How much care ought a man to take of himself, say in a strange inn? Should he put his watch between the sheets to see if they are damp before jumping into bed? Ought he to lock the door? Should he provide himself with matches? Other points will suggest themselves to timid travellers, and on none of them will all the judges of the High Court be found concurring.

The law might very well have been otherwise. The judges might have said in early cases to a defendant in an action for damages for negligence, " As soon as it is established that but for your negligence, that is breach of duty, the accident could not have happened, we will inquire no further. You are admittedly at fault—you have done what you ought not, or you have left undone what you ought; and you shall not be heard to say that he who suffers in consequence of your act or omission might have escaped unhurt if he had taken greater precautions than he did." Had the makers of our Common Law chosen to say this, who could or would have said them nay? But they did not—they laid emphasis on the words *in consequence of*, and took the distinction between proximate and remote causes, with the result that our law reports and newspapers record thousands of cases raising this vexed and vexatious question of contributory negligence.

The remaining question our Common Law asks is this, Had the injured man such a knowledge of the danger or dangers that actually caused the disaster as to create the necessary inference that he voluntarily encountered them? If this question is answered with yes, why then says our Common Law there clearly has been no breach of the duty the employed owed to the particular man who is injured. A barbarous bit of Latinity conveys this dogma, *Volenti non fit injuria*.

This reasoning is not peculiar to, and is indeed no part of, the special law of master and servant, but follows from the general rule of law, that one man cannot sue another in respect of a danger or risk, *not unlawful in itself*, that was visibly apparent and voluntarily encountered by the injured man.

Nobody can say that this is not good sense on the face of it. The keeper of a travelling menagerie engages me to take care of his lions—to feed them and clean out their dens. He shows me over the establishment and acquaints me with its arrangements. I see everything, including the lions, and accept the place. In the course of my duties I irritate one of the lions, and am laid up in consequence. Can it be said that the keeper of the menagerie has been guilty of any breach of duty to me? Or suppose I engage myself to a trade which, though it gives off noxious fumes, is yet a lawful trade (though subject it may be to be abated or restrained as a nuisance), can I be heard to say that my employer has done me harm?

A grown man who voluntarily incurs a known risk must not grumble if he not only runs but realises it. This seems sound sense.

It is when you come to apply it fearlessly

C

to the facts of industrial life as now lived in
smoky England, that you get into difficulty.
Nobody knows the risks to which their labour
exposes them better than the workmen
themselves. These risks are made the subject
matter of sober talk and idle banter. Fami-
liarity with danger breeds a contempt for it.
The bold and skilful workman laughs at risk.
All life is a risk. Death grins at us round
every corner. No Londoner attains middle
age without having been within an inch of
eternity a hundred times whilst traversing our
streets, whilst the hair-breadth escapes we
have witnessed in others would fill a sheet of
The Times. Yet we go mooning about all the
same. The lawyers admit all this, and point
out how the maxim is *Volenti non fit injuria,*
not *scienti.* It is willing, not knowing. But
in sober truth the boundary line between the
two states of mind is not discernible in practice. A man knows of a risk and runs it, is
he not *volens?* Now that Lord Bramwell is
dead, no one is really bold enough to lean
with all his weight upon the doctrine; and if
you read the speeches of the learned lords who
formed the majority in the case of *Smith* v.

Baker (Appeal Cases, 1891, p. 325), and compare them with Lord Bramwell's vigorous confession of an old man's faith in free agency, you will see how judge-made law no less than the law of Parliament obeys the will of circumstance and takes its colour from its surrounding atmosphere. Listen to Lord Herschell, on p. 362 :—

Where then a risk to the employed which may or may not result in an injury has been created or enhanced by the negligence of the employer, does the mere continuance in service with knowledge of the risk preclude the employed, if he suffer from such negligence, from recovering in respect of his employer's breach of duty? I cannot assent to the proposition that the maxim *Volenti non fit injuria* applies to such a case, and that the employer can invoke its aid to protect him from liability for his wrong.

This seems sound sense too, but at the expense of the maxim. If a workman knowing of a risk chooses to remain on and run it, and yet may recover his damages on proving that his employer was negligent in allowing the risk to remain, why should he not also be allowed to recover in cases where the employer's negligence made the accident possible, but was not in the eye of the law its proximate cause? If the maxim *Volenti non fit injuria* is to be whittled down to almost nothing, the doctrine of Contributory Negligence should, I think, share the same fate, and the law be this—the employer who is negligent pays.

There is now left but one lion in my path. I have already referred to *Priestley* v. *Fowler*, which established in the result the following rule of Common Law :—

A servant when he engages to serve a master, undertakes as between himself and his master to run all the ordinary risks of the service, including the risk of negligence upon the part of a fellow servant when he is acting in the discharge of his duty as servant of him who is the common master of both.

This is the beautiful language of a great judge, Sir William Erle. It certainly does not smack of the servants' hall, or the pay office of a Manchester mill. It is of course as sheer invention as the Original Contract between kings and their subjects. No servant ever gave such an undertaking or was asked to do so. Still it is undoubtedly a remarkable fact that, prior to 1836, our Reports contain no case of an action brought by a servant

against his master for damages for injuries
occasioned by the negligence of a fellow-
servant.

Law cases, like lawyers themselves, have
very different fortunes. Most of them blush
unseen in the Law Reports, known only to
the practitioner, and each class of practitioner
knows but his own set of cases. A few are
dragged to the bar of public opinion. *Priestley
v. Fowler* has of late years managed to get
itself a good deal talked about, and has been
denounced at many a trade convention as the
mother of the doctrine of common employment. " Will you vote for the abolition of the
doctrine of common employment ? " was for
years a stock question to the parliamentary
candidate for an industrial community. The
poor fellow, fresh from his club in Pall Mall,
fully primed to state his views as to marriage
with a deceased wife's sister, or the dis-
establishment of the Church, would turn in
his bewilderment to his agent and whisper,
" What in the name of wonder *is* the doctrine
of common employment, and am I in favour
of its abolition ? " But it stood high in public
favour, this doctrine. To declare yourself

against it was, once upon a time, to be a marked man—a cowardly fellow, who was ready to be a mere delegate of the mob. Business, so it was said, could not be carried on without this doctrine. Trade would desert us and fly to countries where, oddly enough, this wonderful doctrine had never been heard of. So it was said; yet when Mr. Asquith's Bill of 1893 proposed to knock it on the head, not so much as a single employer rose in his place to give it decent burial. Never did a doctrine make so poor a show. Religion would blush to own such a doctrine. However, Mr. Asquith's Bill did not become law, and *Priestley* v. *Fowler* is still the law of the land, save as modified in a handful of particular cases by the Employers' Liability Act of 1880.

Let us look at the case as it is to be found in 3 *Meeson* and *Welsby*, p. 1. It is an innocent-looking case. Fowler was a butcher and Priestley one of his servants, who was told by his master to take charge, for the purpose of delivery, of some goods, which were in one of the butcher's vans under the control of and driven by another of the butcher's servants.

In the course of the journey the van broke down, and Priestley fractured his thigh. A Lincolnshire jury, thinking it plain that the van was over-loaded, awarded Priestley £100 ; but on motion for arrest of judgment the verdict was disturbed, and Priestley got nothing, the Court being of opinion that the action was not maintainable.

Lord Abinger's judgment is worth reading.

It is admitted that there is no precedent for the present action by a servant against a master. We are therefore to decide the question upon general principles, and in doing so we are at liberty to look at the consequences of a decision the one way or the other.

If the master be liable to the servant in this action, the principle of that liability will be found to carry us to an alarming extent. He who is responsible by his general duty or by the terms of his contract for all the consequences of negligence in a matter in which he is the principal, is responsible for the negligence of all his inferior agents. If the owner of the carriage is therefore responsible for the sufficiency of his carriage to his servant, he is responsible for the negligence of his coach-maker or his harness-maker or his coachman. The footman therefore who rides behind the carriage may have an action against his master for a defect in the carriage owing to the negligence of the coachmaker, or for a defect in the harness arising from the negligence of the harness-maker, or for drunkenness, neglect, or want of skill in the coachman. Nor is there any reason why the principle should not, if applicable in this class of cases, extend to many others. The master for example would be liable to the servant for the negligence of the chambermaid for putting him into a damp bed, for that of the upholsterer for sending in a crazy bedstead whereby he was made to fall down while asleep and injure himself, for the negligence of the cook in not properly cleaning the copper vessels used in the kitchen, of the butcher in supplying the family with meat of a quality injurious to the health, of the builder for a defect in the foundation of the house whereby it fell and injured both the master and the servant by the ruins.

The inconvenience, not to say the absurdity, of these consequences, affords a sufficient argument against the application of this principle to the present case. But in truth the mere relation of the master and the servant never can imply an obligation on the part of the master to take more care of the servant than he may reasonably be expected to do of himself. He is no doubt bound to provide for the safety of his servant in the course of his employment, to the best of his judgment, information and belief. The servant is not bound to risk his safety in the service of his master, and may if he thinks fit decline any service in which he reasonably apprehends injury to himself ; and in most of the cases in which danger may be incurred, if not in all, he is just as likely to be acquainted with the probability and extent of it as the master. In that sort of employment especially which is described in the declaration in this case, the plaintiff must have known as well as his master, and probably better, whether the van was sufficient, whether it was overloaded, and whether it was likely to carry him safely. In fact to allow this sort of action to prevail would be an encouragement to the servant to omit that diligence and caution which he is

in duty bound to exercise on the behalf of his master,
to protect him against the misconduct or negligence of
others who serve him ; and which diligence and caution,
while they protect the master, are a much better
security against any injury the servant may sustain by
the negligence of others engaged under the same master
than any recourse against his master for damages could
possibly afford.

We are therefore of opinion that the judgment ought
to be arrested.

This, then, is that *Priestley* v. *Fowler* of
which Lord Esher, in his evidence before a
House of Commons Committee, said : " I think
it may be suggested that the law as to non-
liability of masters with regard to fellow-
servants arose principally from the ingenuity
of Lord Abinger, in suggesting analogies in
the case of *Priestley* v. *Fowler.*"

It is not at first sight a very striking case,
and it is plain from the analogies, the terrify-
ing illustrations, of the great advocate who
decided it, that he had not in his mind industrial so much as domestic and quasi-
domestic employments. It may very well be
that if a sleepy housemaid leaves a coal-scuttle
on the staircase, over which next morning
" Bibulous the butler, with calm brows slightly
arched," breaks his leg ; the Courts hear no-

thing about it, for is not Bibulous carried to his apartment, nursed with devotion by the housemaids, attended by the family surgeon, with his wages running all the time ? What damage in money has he sustained ?

The principle that undoubtedly lay concealed in *Priestley* v. *Fowler* was not plainly made manifest in England (though in America it bore its fruit earlier) until 1850, when in the case of *Hutchinson* v. *the York, Newcastle and Berwick Railway*, 5 Exchequer 343, it was held on the authority of *Priestley* v. *Fowler* that the widow of a railway servant could not recover damages under Lord Campbell's Act for the loss of her husband, which was occasioned by the negligence of the servants of the company creating a collision. Baron Alderson said, p. 351 :—

Hutchinson in the discharge of his duty as one of the servants of the Company had put himself into one of their railway carriages under the guidance of others of their servants and by the neglect of those other servants whilst they were engaged together with him on one common service, the accident occurred. This was a risk which Hutchinson must be taken to have agreed to run when he entered into the defendants' service, for the consequences of which therefore they are not responsible.

Here we have the doctrine of common employment naked and unashamed. It is no longer a question of two carpenters working at the same bench, two women grinding at one mill, each able to keep an eye on the other; it is now only a matter of a common paymaster. The judges have not lacked courage in their application of the doctrine to the facts of our industrial and railway systems. Mr. Bevan, in his elaborate treatise on the *Law of Negligence*, Vol. I., p. 804, has collected the cases from which we learn that a labourer is a fellow-servant with an engine-driver and with an inspector, a platelayer with the guard of a train, a scaffolder with a builder's manager, a miner with an underlooker, the manager of a lucifer match manufactory with a boy at five shillings a week, a carpenter on the roof of a station with the men shifting a locomotive engine below.

A case which excited a good deal of attention was decided in 1865, and held that a miner was a fellow-servant with the certificated manager of a colliery appointed pursuant to a statutory obligation; and therefore, though the miner was killed by the negligence of the manager, the widow could recover nothing from the colliery proprietors (*Howells* v. *Landore Siemen's Steel Co.*, 10 L.R. Q.B. 62).

Certainly the force of logic could no farther go.

The whole reasoning of the subject may be found in the speeches of the noble lords who decided the cases of *Bartonshill Coal Company* v. *Reid*, and the same company v. *McGuire*, both reported by Macqueen, Vol. III., pp. 266 and 300 (1858), and of *Wilson* v. *Merry*, 1 L.R. Scotch App. 326 (1868). These cases thrust the doctrine of common employment down the throats of the Scottish judges.

It would be absurd to say that the doctrine is a ridiculous one. Had it been so it never would have commended itself to the minds of so many great judges. When you once begin inventing terms for other people's contracts there is usually a good deal to be said in favour of your fancy. Supposing our judges had decided, as they have in France, that it is an implied term of every contract of service that the master shall insure his servant against all accidents in the course of the employment which are not solely attributable to the

servant's own negligence or to unforeseen and
most unlikely occurrences,—who would have
found fault with this fiction? When you are
writing a novel you may make it long or
short, merry or sad, as you please.

THE EMPLOYERS' LIABILITY UNDER THE ACT OF 1880

In my first Lecture I made a survey, necessarily hasty and far from exhaustive, but I hope accurate within its limits, of the liability at Common Law of the Employer towards the Employed to pay damages for injuries sustained by the latter in the course of their Employment. From that survey it was made plain—and I sought to emphasise the fact as much as possible—that by the Common Law the subject under discussion is a branch of the Law of Negligence; and therefore that no man, be his relation to the injured man what it may, can be required to put his hand into his pocket and pay damages for that injury unless it has been, or by admission can be, proved that the injury was occasioned by a breach of some legal duty which he owed to the injured man. Negligence, we discovered, was the absence of that amount of care which in the circumstances of the case ought as a matter of legal duty to have been present. This then is the basis of the Law of Liability. Negligence, i.e., a breach of duty. No breach of duty, no Negligence. No Negligence, no liability. On this basis our masterful and masterly Judges have built up a huge superstructure of Law which, so far as it affects Master and Servant, I considered under the three heads of *Contributory Negligence*, *Consent* or *Volenti non fit Injuria*, and the much canvassed doctrine of *Common Employment*. The two first named are, every one must admit, legitimate applications of the law of Negligence to particular sets of circumstances. They may savour of subtlety, they may perhaps inquire too curiously into the springs of action and the birth of motive, but no one will deny that if a man rushes into danger, and neglecting the ordinary precautions which sensible men in like circumstances are accustomed to take, suffers a mischance, it is not

unreasonable to hold that the ill which has
overtaken him is due to his own negligence,
and not to that of the man who created or
permitted the danger to exist. So too if a
grown-up man has a danger pointed out to
him, or discovers it for himself, and yet con-
tinues to labour on in its vicinity, there is
nothing irrational in the inference that he
assented to run the risk, preferring that risk
to the certainty of losing his employment.
Yet if he did so assent, it is perhaps strain-
ing the law of Negligence to say that his
employer is guilty of a breach of duty to him
if the contemplated risk is not only run but
realised.

The doctrine of *Common Employment* has
no connection in reason with the law of Negligence, but is merely a contrivance to prevent
the Common Law having full swing. It cuts
down the formula *Respondeat Superior* (which
as we saw was itself a violent extension of the
moral basis of Negligence), by holding that
every servant on entering into a contract of
service undertakes as a risk incident to his
employment the chance of being injured by
the negligence of his fellow-servants.

It was this last named doctrine, and the lengths to which the Judges carried it, that first aroused the discontent of the leaders of the Trades Unions now first escaping from the meshes of the Law of Conspiracy. Public attention was directed to judicial decisions. The case already quoted of *Howells* v. *Landore Siemen's Steel Company*, 10 L.R., Q.B., 62, where the certificated manager of a mine was allowed to kill a miner with impunity was much animadverted upon ; as also was a case decided so long ago as 1865 of *Morgan* v. *the Vale of Neath Railway Company*, 1 L.R., Q.B., 149, where a carpenter who was injured by the carelessness of some of the Railway Company's porters who knocked down the scaffold on which he was standing, was held to be without any right of action, Chief Baron Pollock observing :—

It appears to me that we should be letting in a flood of litigation were we to decide the present case in favour of the plaintiff. For if a carpenter's employment is to be distinguished from that of the porters employed by the same company it will be sought to split up the *employés* in every large establishment into different departments of service, although the common object of their employment, however different, is but the furtherance of the business of the master; yet it might be said with truth that no two had a common immediate object. This shows that we must not over refine but look at the common object, and not at the common immediate object.

The Chief Baron could hardly have said less in 1865 ; but his remarks did not carry conviction with them, and from that time forward the movement began to get this doctrine modified if not abolished. In 1876 a Committee of the House of Commons was appointed to inquire into the relations of master and servant. It was reappointed the following year, and took a great deal of interesting evidence, which is duly recorded in the Parliamentary papers of the period. The Committee presented their Report and recommended by way of amendment of the Common Law, *first*, that in cases where the employer had delegated his authority to another, an injured man should not be considered as the fellow-servant of the master's delegate ; and, *secondly*, that generally the doctrine of common employment should only apply in cases where the servant could by personal observation or complaint control the conduct of his fellow-servant.

Three years later came the Employers' Liability Act, 1880, which was intended to give effect to the recommendations of the Committee and to remedy the injustice of which the working population had complained.

This Act is a very good, that is a very bad, example of our method of driving our legal system in double harness. We have always with us our Common Law as it is from term to term revealed to us in the judgments of our most eminent judges (for the less eminent judges rarely make law, their efforts in that direction being usually nipped in the bud by the Appeal Court) ; and whenever any particular decision or class of decision excites an unusual amount of disgust, popular disfavour or class animosity—why then, after much loose talk in the newspapers and some investigation before a Parliamentary Committee, a statute is passed amending, or purporting to amend, the particular grievance complained of. Our Common Law and our Statute Law are thus inextricably entangled.

Turning to the Act of 1880, we find it intituled, " An Act to extend and regulate the

Liability of Employers to make Compensation for Personal Injuries suffered by Workmen in their Service."

We may note here our national passion for using two words instead of one. The Act does *extend* the liability of employers beyond their Common Law liability; but it is incorrect to say it *regulates* the liability of employers, since all it does is to make an employer liable *under the Act* in certain specified cases which at Common Law imposed no liability. In those cases the Act provides a remedy, limits the compensation and establishes a procedure, but in all other cases it leaves the Common Law liability where it found it. If a working man who is within the Act has sustained an injury and thinks he can bring his case within any one of the five sets of circumstances specified in the Act, he can take his proceedings as by the Act directed. But if he cannot do this, or if he does not choose to do this, the Common Law of England remains very much at his service.

The Act does however increase an employer's liability. What is the measure of that increase? The measure is to be found in the concluding words of Clause 1 :—

The workman, or in case the injury results in death, the legal personal representatives of the workman, and any persons entitled in case of death, shall have the same right of compensation and remedies against the employer as if the workman had not been a workman of nor in the service of the employer, nor engaged in his work.

These words taken by themselves are supposed to abolish and have been held to abolish the doctrine of common employment in the cases specified in the various subsections of Clause 1.

The criticism of Mr. Justice Cave upon the language of the Act must be admitted to be sound. " I agree," said Mr. Justice Cave, in *Griffiths* v. *The Earl of Dudley*, 9 Q. B. Div. 365,

that the language of Section 1 of the Employers' Liability Act has not been felicitously chosen. Taking the language in its apparently literal sense the plaintiff must be regarded as a stranger. If he is to be taken as not being a workman of nor in the service of the employer, nor engaged in his work, it follows that he is on the premises as a trespasser or bare licensee. He is not there under contract, nor in the performance of any work in which the employer and he are mutually interested ; so that in the majority of cases no action

could be maintained. But I think the real meaning of
the Legislature is this ; as far back as the date of the
decision in *Priestley* v. *Fowler*, the law was that the
workman could not recover for injuries sustained by
him through the negligence of a fellow-servant. In
Priestley v. *Fowler* this rule was said to be founded
upon an implied contract between master and workman,
that the master should not be liable. The Courts of
Common Law have always felt hesitation in holding
that there could be any right of action otherwise than
arising out of contract or tort. They therefore applied
the doctrine of implied contract—the effect of which,
so far as a man's legal liability was concerned, was
much the same as if there had been an express contract.
The doctrine was extended by *Wilson* v. *Merry* to
injuries caused to a workman by a foreman, or person
occupying a position of superintendence, in the same
employment. The Employers' Liability Act was
passed to remove the difficulty arising from the decision
in *Wilson* v. *Merry*. The effect of it is that the
workman may bring his action in five specified cases,
and the employer shall not be able to say in answer
that the plaintiff occupied the position of workman in
his service, and must therefore be taken to have
impliedly contracted not to hold the employer liable.
In other words the legal result of the plaintiff being a
workman shall not be that he has impliedly contracted
to bear the risks of the employment.

This then is the benevolent interpretation
placed by the judges upon the infelicitous
language of the statute, and we are therefore
safe in taking it that the doctrine of common
employment is abolished in the five cases

specified in the first clause; although, were the words of the clause which I have quoted made to bear their true meaning, the position of the workman under them would have been hardly improved, since he would have been, as Mr. Justice Cave points out, relegated to the position either of a trespasser or of a bare licensee, and only invested with the meagre rights belonging to such persons.

This, then, is the total outcome of the Act. It says that in certain cases and in certain circumstances Lord Abinger's doctrine shall not deprive an injured workman of his right to damages. This, you will remember, was one of the things the public had it on its mind to do, though the Parliamentary Committee which reported in the way I have before quoted certainly never contemplated the particular phraseology of the Act.

One word as to the workmen within the Act. The Act includes railway servants and any person to whom the Employers and Workmen's Act, 1875, applies, namely, any person who being a labourer, servant in husbandry, journeyman, artificer, handicraftsman, miner, or otherwise engaged in manual labour, whether under the age of twenty-one years or above that age, has entered into or works under a contract with an employer, whether the contract be made before or after 1875, be express or implied, oral or in writing, and be a contract of service or a contract personally to execute any work or labour. Seamen and sea apprentices are expressly excluded from the Employers and Workmen's Act, 1875, as also are domestic or menial servants ; consequently, neither seamen, sea apprentices, nor domestic or menial servants are within the Employers' Liability Act, 1890, but agricultural labourers are within the Act, though its terms have but small application to them.

I will now examine the specified cases to which the doctrine of *Priestley* v. *Fowler* need no longer apply. I say " need no longer apply " because unless the workman avails himself of the Act it does still apply.

In order to find out what these specified cases are you have to cut up the Act into little bits—I mean literally not critically—and paste them in their proper places. Unless you do this the Act defies you.

Clause 1 enumerates five cases where if a

workman sustains personal injury the doctrine of common employment need not apply. But then in Clause 2 it proceeds to state certain circumstances when, notwithstanding Clause 1, the doctrine shall apply. In order therefore to understand what the cases are to which in practice the Act applies, you have to read into the subsections of Clause 1 the subsections of Clause 2. I proceed to do this.

When after the commencement of this Act personal injury is caused to a workman (1) by reason of any defect in the condition of the ways, works, machinery, or plant connected with or used in the business of the employer, which defect arose from or had not been discovered or remedied owing to the negligence of the employer or of some person in the service of the employer and entrusted by him with the duty of seeing that the ways, works, machinery, or plant were in proper order, *then the doctrine of common employment is not to apply* unless the workman knew of the defect which caused his injury and failed within a reasonable time to give or cause to be given information thereof to the employer or some person superior to himself in the service of the

employer unless the workman was aware that
the employer or such superior already knew of
the said defect.

This, then, is the first of the five specified
cases; and we are now (I hope) able to
appreciate the scope and purpose of the Act
and to perceive how strictly limited that scope
and purport is.

First we see that the employer must either
be negligent himself or negligent in the
person of another to whom he has entrusted
the particular duty referred to in the sub-
section. *Secondly* we see that the law of
contributory negligence remains unaltered,
since in the eye of the law negligence is not
actionable unless it is the proximate cause of
the accident; and *Thirdly* we notice that
knowledge of the defect and failure within a
reasonable time to give notice of it will
destroy the right to damage, unless the workman was aware that the employer already
knew of the defect. What then is new about
this law?

There was always, and still is, a liability at
common law on the part of the employer or
master, to provide and maintain proper

materials, machinery and plant for the work
in and about which the servants are engaged.
Bartonshill Coal Company v. *Reid*, 3 Macqueen, 288 ; *Wilson* v. *Merry*, L.R. Scotch
Appeals 332, 344 ; and a master or employer
who fails in this duty is liable at common
law to his servant or workman, unless the
latter knew of, and therefore by inference
of law acquiesced in, the dangerous condition
of things.

The language of the subsection under consideration probably does add a little to the
obligation of an employer in the matter of
ways, works, machinery or plant ; but if it
does, this new obligation arises from the
precision of the language of the subsection.
But the real novelty in the law is the liability
imposed upon the employer to answer for the
negligence of the person in his service to
whom he had entrusted the duty of seeing
that the ways, works, machinery or plant
were in proper condition. At common law
no such liability existed.

Subsection 2 is as follows. Where after
the commencement of this Act personal
injury is caused to a workman (2) by

reason of the negligence of any person in the service of the employer who has *any* superintendence entrusted to him whilst in the exercise of such superintendence, *then the doctrine of common employment is not to apply*, unless the workman knew of the negligence which caused his injury, and failed within a reasonable time to give, or cause to be given, information thereof to the employer or some person superior to himself in the service of the employer, unless the workman was aware that the employer or such superior already knew of the said negligence. This is new law, and satisfies the first of the two recommendations of the Parliamentary Committee.

The third of the specified cases is as follows. Where after the commencement of this Act personal injury is caused to a workman (3) by reason of the neglect of any person in the service of the employer to whose orders or directions the workman at the time of the injury was bound to conform, and did conform, where such injury resulted from his having so conformed, *then the doctrine of common employment is not to apply*, unless

the workman knew of the negligence which
caused his injury, and failed as aforesaid.
This also is new law.

The fourth of the five cases specified by the
Act is as follows. Where after the commencement of this Act personal injury is caused to
a workman (4) by reason of the act or
omission of any person in the service of the
employer done or made in obedience to rules
or bye-laws of the employer, or in obedience
to particular instructions given by any person
delegated with the authority of the employer
in that behalf, *then the doctrine of common
employment is not to apply*, unless the injury
resulted from some impropriety or *defect* in
the rules, bye-laws, or instructions therein
mentioned; provided that where a rule or
bye-law has been approved, or has been
accepted as a proper rule or bye-law, by one
of Her Majesty's Principal Secretaries of
State, or by the Board of Trade, or any other
Department of the Government under or by
virtue of any Act of Parliament, it shall not
be deemed for the purposes of this Act to be
an improper or defective rule or bye-law.
This is the only one of the five cases specified

by the Act which is not based upon the
negligence of the employer, or of some
person to whom the employer has entrusted
the work in question. If the employer's rules
or bye-laws, or the particular instructions
given by any person to whom the employer
had delegated his authority, occasioned the
accident, the employer is responsible, unless
the rule or bye-law has been approved or
accepted by the specified authorities or one of
them. This also is new law.

The fifth and last of the specified cases is as
follows. Where after the commencement of
this Act personal injury is caused to a workman (5) by reason of the negligence of any
person in the service of the employer who has
the charge or control of any signal points,
Locomotive Engine or Train upon a railway,
*then the doctrine of common employment
is not to apply*, unless the workman knew of
the negligence which caused his injury and
failed as aforesaid. This also is new law, and
was framed for the purpose of getting rid of
the hardship of such cases as *M'Eniry* v.
Waterford and Kilkenny Ry. Co., 8 Ir.
Common Law Reports 312 (1858); *Waller* v.

South Eastern Ry. Co., 2 H. and C. 102 (1863); *Loregrove* v. *London Brighton and South Coast Ry. Co.*, and *Gallagher* v. *Piper* 16 C.B. N.S. 669 (1864); *Morgan* v. *Vale of Neath Ry. Co.*, L.R. 1 Q.B. 149 (1865); *Tunney* v. *Midland Ry. Co.*, L.R. 1 C.P. 291 (1866).

It would be useless in this place to consider one by one the very numerous cases that have been decided under this Act, and which already cover it as it were with a cloud. The public is apt to be unreasonably indignant with the multiplicity of cases, and to assert that their existence proves the incompetency of the Legislature; but if liability is to depend on negligence it must be determined by circumstances; and who can stereotype endless circumstance, or prevent one case differing from another? On the whole the Judges have given the Act a fair chance, though some County Court Judges are accused of being hostile to it; and the amount of litigation it has given rise to, however much to be regretted, cannot be said to be extraordinary. As compared for example with such Acts as those regulating the law relating to Bills of Sale, the Employers' Liability Act of 1880,—tough reading to the working man as

Sir Frederick Pollock has declared it to be—is
quite a model of lucid draughtsmanship.

Whether the Act carried out to the full the
recommendations of the Parliamentary Committee is doubtful. So far as the Act provides
for the responsibility of the Employer in the
case of persons to whom he had delegated his
authority, it seems to have done all the Committee recommended; but it was no doubt
intended by that body that the doctrine of
common employment should be severely re-
stricted to those cases where the servant had
an opportunity of observing and complaining
of the conduct of his fellow-servant. The Act
contains no such general restriction, although
no doubt it goes a long way in that direction.
The only servants whose neglect will render
their employer liable to a fellow servant are :

(1) Persons entrusted by the employer with
the duty of seeing that the ways, works,
machinery and plant connected with or used
in the employer's business are in proper order.

(2) Persons who have any superintendence
entrusted to them by their employer.

(3) Persons authorised to give the order or
direction which occasioned the injury.

(4) Persons acting in obedience to rules or bye-laws obedience to which occasioned the accident, unless such rules or bye-laws have been approved by the Home Secretary or the Board of Trade.

(5) Persons obeying particular instructions given by any persons duly authorised in that behalf by the employer; and

(6) Persons in charge or control of any Signal Points, Locomotive Engine or Train upon a Railway.

The compensation recoverable under the Act is not to exceed an equivalent to the estimated earnings during the three years preceding the injury of a person in the same grade, employed during those years in the like employment and in the district in which the workman is employed at the time of the injury. The fourth Section of the Act imposes certain limits of time for recovery of compensation by providing that no action under the Act for compensation should be maintainable unless notice of the injury is given within six weeks, and the action is commenced within six months from the occurrence of the accident causing the injury, or in case of death within twelve months

E

from the time of death. In the case of death, however, there is a proviso that the want of such notice shall be no bar to the action if the Judge shall be of opinion that there was reasonable excuse therefor. All Actions under the Act are by the sixth Section to be brought in the County Court, subject to removal to a superior Court under certain conditions. On the trial of the action a jury may be demanded if notice of demand is given in writing to the Registrar of the Court fifteen clear days at least before the return day.

The Act says nothing about contracting out. But in the year 1882, in the well known case of *Griffiths* v. *The Earl of Dudley*, 9 Q.B.D. 357, where it was held that a workman had contracted with his employer for himself and his representatives and any person entitled in case of death not to claim any compensation under the Act for personal injury whether resulting in death or not, it was decided that such a contract was not against public policy, and that the workman's widow suing for damages under Lord Campbell's Act was bound by it. The authority of this case has never been questioned.

This Act is at present the only statutory modification of the Common Law on any of the subjects I have discussed which exists.

(For copy of the Act see Appendix B.)

FOREIGN LAW AND SYSTEMS OF INSURANCE

ON the Continent of Europe the law as to Employers' liability as distinguished from any scheme for compulsory insurance of workmen against accidents is substantially the same as our own Common Law, that is to say it is a branch of the law of negligence.

In regard to some special trades and occupations there have been in many of the different countries of Europe special legislation affecting Employers' responsibility; but, apart from these enactments, the law of Europe is for the most part in accordance with the principles of the French Civil Code, which contains the following Articles :—

Art. 1382.—Any action whatever of a man which

causes an injury to another obliges the person *by whose fault* the injury has occurred to repair it.

Art. 1383.—Everybody is responsible for the injury he has caused, not only by his action but also by his negligence and imprudence.

Art. 1384.—A man is responsible not only for the injury he causes by his own action but also for that which is caused by the action of persons for whom he is answerable or of things in his charge.

The father or the mother after the decease of the husband are responsible for the injury caused by their children who live with them, being minors.

Masters and employers, for the injury caused by their servants and overseers in the performance of the functions in which they have employed them.

Tutors and artisans, for the injury caused by their pupils or apprentices during the time they are under their supervision.

This responsibility is incurred unless the father, mother, tutor, or artisan prove that they could not prevent the action which gave rise to the responsibility.

This law, which is more than a hundred years old, still remains the law of France and also the law of Belgium; although in both countries there is a movement in the direction of what may be conveniently called the German system of Insurance against accidents.

The cases in France and Belgium under this law have been numerous, and proceed upon the same lines as our English decisions, except that their general tendency is more favourable to

the workman. Nothing is known abroad of
the doctrine of common employment, nor has
the law of proximate causes or contributory
negligence been scientifically developed as in
England; and generally speaking it may be
said that under the Code Napoleon and the
decisions of the Courts applying its principles,
the employer in France or Belgium undertakes
by virtue of the contract between himself and
his workman to watch over the safety of the
workman in performance of the work for
which he is employed, but does not guarantee
him against all kinds of dangers inherent to
the work unless the accident has arisen through
some fault or want of oversight on the part of
the employer, and the *onus* of proving this
fault falls upon the workman. In a case
decided in France in the course of this year
it was held that the employer is free from
liability where the accident arises from what
in England is called the act of God, and in
France is called *vis major*, or in other words
where the accident has been produced by one
of those phenomena that science is unable to
explain or by circumstances contrary to the
ordinary course of things and which in the

present state of industry upset the measures
of precaution required by prudence and fore-
sight.

In Austria the liability of employers to
compensate workmen injured in their service
is regulated by the ordinary Civil Law, which
provides simply that the employer is responsible for those accidents occurring to his
workmen which arise from his personal negligence; and in Austria an employer is not
responsible for the acts or omissions of those
to whom he has delegated his authority unless
it can be proved that he has made a wrongful
selection or has improperly retained in his
service a person by whose fault any accident
has occurred.

In Italy, Sweden, Holland, Denmark, Spain
and Russia it may be generally stated that the
only liability of the employer is under what I
will call the Common Law, and that the workman must in each case discharge the *onus* cast
upon him of proving negligence. There is
however, as may be seen from a Report of
Her Majesty's Representatives Abroad on the
Laws Regulating the Liability of Employers
in Foreign Countries, presented to both Houses

of Parliament in June, 1886 (Commercial, No. 21 [1886]), a very noticeable disposition or tendency throughout Europe to shift the ground from liability for negligence to insurance against accidents ; or, in other words, to follow the example, with such modifications as may be suggested in each country which Germany has set to Europe.

In many of the various States now forming the German Empire there were to be found existing for considerable periods of time systems or institutions sometimes guaranteed, and in all cases recognised by the State, of sick insurance for workpeople whereby funds were provided to keep a man and his belongings "a going concern" during sickness. Of course in the case of an industrial population one great cause of sickness is accident.

It would only be to trouble you with useless detail to attempt, however shortly, to give an account of the various Acts of the Legislature, which in the German States, and particularly in Prussia, were from time to time passed, dealing both with accidents and insurance. So long ago as 1854 it was made compulsory in Prussia for every workman to belong to a sick relief society, to which the employers were also compelled by law to contribute ; and in 1871 an Act was passed in Prussia making employers personally liable in most of the dangerous trades and callings for all accidents, except those occasioned by culpable negligence. Contracting out was not allowed. Mr. Charles Green in an interesting paper read before the Manchester Insurance Institute, on the 8th of December, 1896, states that this Act failed because of the cost of its procedure.

In 1881, a Bill was introduced in the Reichstag which proposed to create the necessary machinery to insure workmen in railways, factories, and mines, against every kind of accident, and divided the premiums necessary to secure this object in equal thirds between the employer, the insured, and the State. The Socialistic party sought to extend the measure to all trades and employments, and to throw upon the employer the whole burden of the scheme. In the course of the discussion the State liability was got rid of, and the premiums were divided between the employer and the workman, in the proportions of two to one. In this shape the Bill passed the Reichstag, but never became law.

The existing German scheme, which consists of two sister measures, the Sickness Insurance Act and the Accidents Insurance Act, came into joint operation in 1885. The Sickness Insurance Bill was the first to pass. Amended at different times these two Acts still remain in full force, and together form that German scheme of which we are now hearing so much.

Stating their effect very shortly, always bear in mind that the Sickness Insurance Act is compulsory, and by its provisions every working man or woman earning wages is obliged to join some recognised club or society; and as all societies are affiliated together, a member of one can transfer himself to another as he moves about from place to place. On the funds of these societies, which may for all purposes be considered one, devolves the full burden of providing the money necessary to keep the insured man or woman who has become by an accident of any kind incapable of attending to his or her labour for a period of thirteen weeks, if the effects of the accident so long continue. If at the end of that time the workman is still incapable, he is cast upon the funds provided under the Accident Insurance Act, which allots to him compensation according to a fixed scale.

Mr. Green, in the interesting pamphlet I have already quoted from, speaks of this German scheme as being " the very pinnacle of State Socialism." But is it? My notion of Socialism is, a scheme under the terms of which the bill for everything is sent in to everybody. Who pays the bill in Germany? Let us look at the system a little closer.

Under the Sickness Insurance Act the obligation to insure his workpeople is cast upon the employer, who no doubt pays the whole of the premiums in the first instance, but is permitted to deduct the workpeople's share from their wages. And what is the workpeople's share? Two-thirds, the remaining third being paid by the employer himself.

Under this Act (the Sickness Insurance Act) the vast majority of the accidents which occur in Germany are fully dealt with. Out of the 310,000 odd accidents of which notice was given in 1895, only 75,000 remained to be treated under the Accident Insurance Act. In other words the great majority of the accidents occuring in the industrial occupations of Germany yielded to a treatment of thirteen weeks ; and during that time the working classes themselves contributed two-thirds of their expenses, and the employer the remaining third.

The Accident Insurance Act takes up the cases which do not yield to a thirteen week treatment, and imposes upon the employer the obligation of providing the whole of the funds necessary to provide the moneys payable under the tariff created by the Act. The general public, be it observed, does not contribute a penny piece to the fund.

We therefore see that for the first thirteen weeks of an accident the workpeople pay two-thirds and the employer one-third, and in cases requiring further assistance the employers pay all. I do not think the expression State Socialism can properly be applied to any such system as this.

Just as under the Sickness Insurance Act every workman is compelled to join a sick Society, so under the Accident Insurance Act

every employer of a trade scheduled to the
Act is bound to join a group or corporation of
similar trades; and it is to this group or
corporation that the injured workman looks
for the compensation to which he has become
entitled under the provisions of the Accident
Insurance Act. There are 112 of these Corporations, of which 48 are agricultural and 64
Industrial. Mr. Henry W. Wolff, in his
pamphlet entitled *Employers' Liability: What
ought it to be?* (P. S. King & Son, 1897) gives
some interesting details as to these Corporations. There are, he tells us, six Textile
Corporations, besides one for Silk Weavers and
another for Flax Spinners, eight Iron and Steel
Corporations, and twelve Builders' Corporations. These Corporations have their own
Inspectors, and meet together in annual
congress to discuss their affairs and liabilities,
and to prepare, so Mr. Wolff assures us, model
regulations for the protection of accidents as
well, and also to make representations or
recommendations to the Government with a
view to improving the Act.

The procedure is as follows. First of all
the accident happens doing injury to some-

body. Then there is a police inquiry as to
the fact of the accident. The obligation of
giving notice of the accident to the police is
thrown upon the employer, who has to do so
within two days of its occurrence. The Police
make their inquiry and forward their Report
to the Corporation within three days after
receiving the notice. It then becomes the
duty of the Corporation to award compensation. It does so on its own motion and by its
own authority. If the accident results in
death the Corporation has at once to pay
the workman's funeral expenses, and if
he leaves dependents behind him compensation as awarded. If the accident is not
of a fatal character the Corporation calls
upon the sick fund under the Sickness
Insurance Act to do its part, and the actual
liability of the Accident Insurance Corporation
does not begin until after the expiration of
three months; although,—and this is a point
not to be overlooked,—the Corporation may as
a matter of expediency undertake the healing
of the sick man itself at the earliest possible
date, but at the charges of the Sick Fund.

As the working man is not represented in

the first instance when the Award is made he naturally is dissatisfied with it, and in almost all cases he appeals from the Corporation to a Court composed of two employers and two workmen, presided over by some independent person. From this tribunal there is in many cases a second appeal to the Imperial Insurance Department, the decision of which is final. The Imperial Court is also composed of employers and workmen in equal proportions, with an Imperial Officer as president.

The Awards, whatever they may be, are paid through the Post Office, which at the end of the year sends in its Bill to the different Corporations, who proceed to levy the total amount of their contributions from their members in proportions which depend upon the special danger risk of the individual employer's work, and the total amount of the wages he pays.

From some statistics quoted by Mr. Wolff it appears that the corporation's task of recovering from its individual contributors their proper proportion is far from an easy one; and though the result of the German system as a whole may be to prevent litigation about accidents, it cannot be said to prevent it altogether; for it appears that the Corporation of Hackney Coaches and Carriers in the year 1892 had to sue some 7,000 of its members for their contribution, whilst the Mine Owners' Corporation had over 154 contributions to collect by civil process. However, this is the system.

What does this liability amount to in cash? This is a difficult question to answer. Mr. Wolff says that quarry owners (and quarrying is one of the most dangerous of trades) pay three or four per cent. on their wages, mine owners two per cent., textile industries only about 0·6 per cent., and that taking all the trades altogether the tax amounts to a little over one per cent. on the wages paid.

Another question much controverted is, Does the German system prevent accidents? Speaking *a priori* I should have thought it must have that effect. Here are great Corporations composed of the men who know most about the particular trades grouped together, and familiar with their inherent dangers and risks, and upon these Corporations so composed is flung the whole burden of paying for all

serious accidents happening in the course of
these trades. The Corporations employ their
own Inspectors, and collect and preserve
evidence of accidents and consider how best
accidents may be prevented. The Corporations
have also the power of punishing individual
members against whom there is a bad record
of accidents, by the simple process of increasing
the amount of their contributions. The total
liability imposed by the system, although not
enough to cripple industry, is still sufficiently
large to be a matter of constant anxiety, and
therefore requiring perpetual attention. It
seems hard to resist the conclusion that such a
system must in the long run have a preventive
tendency.

It is also asserted that the Corporations show
praiseworthy anxiety to cure injured persons
as speedily as possible in order to prevent their
coming upon their pension list. The Corporations frequently have their own hospitals, in
which they are willing to receive the injured
man from the first, and where no expense is
spared to cure him. Of course the Sick Fund
has to pay its proportion of these expenses.

Anyhow, there can be no doubt that the

F

German system during the last ten years has been worked, on the whole, satisfactorily, and upon a huge scale. Over 12,000,000 people engaged in agriculture, over 5,000,000 people engaged in Industrial callings, and nearly 3,000,000 people in addition, fall within its scope. The list of killed and wounded and widows, children and dependants who annually receive compensation under the scheme is very large. Mr. Wolff gives many interesting details. The 48 Agricultural Corporations paid in 1895 a great number of marks in compensation to 103,363 injured persons, and also paid for the medical treatment of 12,591 persons ; whilst the 64 Industrial Corporations compensated 148,696 injured persons, and paid for the medical treatment of 23,323.

Austria adopted the German system or one very similar to it in 1887, the main difference being that the joint liability of employers to compensate their workmen is thrown upon the trade within a district and not upon the whole trade throughout the country. Each Province has its own Insurance Institution composed of employers who are liable under the law, but the Provinces may unite if they choose and trades may form their own Insurance groups under certain conditions. The Insurance groups are governed by committees consisting one-third of employers, one-third of workmen, and one-third of members nominated by the Provincial Council. Inquiries are held into every accident by the local authorities with whom the Insurance group may be associated. The appeal from awards made by the Insurance Institutions is to an Arbitration Board composed of a permanent president nominated by the Minister of Justice and four assessors, of whom two are chosen by the Minister of the Interior, one is appointed by the employers, and one by the workmen. If the accident has arisen by the wilful act or default of the employer or his representative, the whole of the payments made to the injured man must be refunded to the Insurance Institution. (See the Report of the Special Commissioner of the *Daily Chronicle*, Feb. 1, 1897.)

Another important distinction between the German and the Austrian systems is that in Austria the period of Sick Fund illness is limited to four weeks instead of thirteen.

In France the subject has been under dis-

cussion for a very long time, in fact ever since
1881. In 1884 a Bill more or less upon the
German system came on for discussion in the
Chamber of Deputies. M. Treitt thus describes
the debates which then took place :—

Les débats ont été vifs et animés ; tout le monde
s'est dit l'ami des ouvriers ; mais le principe de la
responsabilité *absolue* des patrons ou employeurs a été
combattu avec énergie. Il a paru exorbitant que l'on
renversât en faveur l'axiôme que le demandeur est
obligé de faire la preuve de son action (*actori incumbit
probatio*) et que l'employeur fût responsable *ipso facto*
de tous les accidents quel qu'ils fussent et que se fût
à lui à faire la preuve négative qu'il n'est pas la cause
de l'accident.

None however of the various schemes that
have from time to time been before the French
Chamber have become law ; but there is now,
and has been for some time past in draft, a
complete scheme of insurance against accidents,
a full print of which may be seen in the
Parliamentary Paper, Foreign Office, 1892,
Miscellaneous Series, No. 258, page 148.

I will only refer to a few of the principal
Articles.

Art. 1.—All accidents happening by and during the
performance of their duties to workmen and employés
engaged in building works, factories, manufactures,
yards, transport loading and unloading of merchandise,

public warehouses, mines, mining stores, quarries, and generally in all establishments or branches thereof in which explosive materials are manufactured or employed, or where use is made of steam engines or machines worked by elementary powers (air, water, steam, gas, hot air, electricity, &c.), or by animals, give right in favour of the sufferer or his representatives to compensation, the importance and character of which are hereinafter determined.

This provision is applicable to workmen and employers engaged in enterprises and works connected with the State, the departments, districts, and public establishments.

Art. III.—When the accident causes permanent and absolute incapacity to work the sufferer is entitled to a life annuity equal to two-thirds of his annual wages.

Blindness, the complete loss of the use of two limbs or any incurable infirmity which renders the workman unable to work and provide for his maintenance, are considered as permanent and absolute incapacity to work.

Art. VIII.—In all accidents which have caused incapacity to work during more than three days, the head of the establishment shall bear the expense of medical attendance and medicines. He shall also pay during the illness arising from the accident a sum equal to one-half of the sufferer's wages, on condition that such sum does not exceed 3 fr. 50 c. per diem.

The head of the establishment is only responsible for this compensation for a period not exceeding 30 days from the date of the accident. After the thirtieth day, if the sufferer be not in a fit state to return to his work, the temporary indemnity above provided and cost of attendance and medicines shall be at the charge of the district. The head of the establishment shall, however, continue to provide them up to the time when a definite decision has been pronounced by competent jurisdiction, but as an advance only, and at the expense of the district which shall reimburse him.

This temporary compensation shall be paid from the date of the accident at the usual periods of payment of wages, and at the latest every 15 days.

Art. IX.—Heads of establishments may relieve themselves of the obligation to pay the cost of the illness and temporary compensation during the first 30 days following the accident if they can prove—

(1) That they have at their own cost founded special benefit funds, or have associated their workmen to approved or authorised mutual aid societies.

(2) That such funds or societies are bound to pay, independently of the treatment of the wounded, a compensation equal to one-half of their daily wages, on condition that this indemnity shall not be obliged to exceed 3 fr. 50 c. per diem during the illness, or at least during the first 30 days.

Art. XII.—Every accident causing incapacity to work, and happening in establishments of the class mentioned in Art. I., shall be declared by the head of the establishment or his representative.

This declaration shall be made within 48 hours of the occurrence to the mayor of the district, who shall draw up an official report in the form to be settled by a Ministerial Decree.

The head of the establishment shall annex to this declaration a medical certificate setting forth the state of the injured person, the probable consequences of the accident, and the date when it may be possible to learn the positive result.

A voucher for the declaration and medical certificate shall be immediately given by the mayor to the deponent.

Similar declarations and productions of certificates may be made by the injured man or his representatives.

Art. XIII.—When the injuries appear likely to become fatal or to entail permanent incapacity for work, the mayor shall send copies of the declarations and medical certificate to the justice of the peace for the district.

Within 24 hours of the receipt of such notice the justice of the peace shall institute an inquiry for the purpose of learning—

(1) The cause, nature, and circumstances of the accident.

(2) The names of the sufferers.

(3) The kind of injuries sustained.

(4) The place where the killed or the wounded are to be found.

(5) The relatives of the sufferers who may present claims for compensation.

(6) The daily and annual wages of the sufferers.

Art. XVII.—Disputes between sufferers from accidents, the heads of establishments, or the district with regard to temporary compensation, medical attendance, cost of medicines, and funeral expenses, shall be decided without appeal by the justice of the peace of the district where the accident occurred.

Art. XVIII.—With regard to the other compensations provided for by the present law, within eight days of the reception of the documents relating to the inquiry the President of the Civil Tribunal shall convene the injured person or his representatives, the head of the establishment and the representative of the district. If the parties agree, the amount of the compensation shall be definitely settled by an order of the President, who delivers an act to this effect.

When the parties do not agree the dispute shall be

settled at the chief town of the district where the accident occurred by a Court composed of three heads of establishments and three workmen assembled before the President of the Tribunal, or in his absence before the judge appointed by him.

Art. XXVII.—The decision of the Court of Arbitration can only be appealed against by a petition of appeal, and then only for excess of power or violation of law. The appeal must be made by declaration at the registry of the Civil Tribunal within 15 days from the date of the decision.

Art. XXX.—Neither of the compensations settled by the present law may be allowed to the injured persons who intentionally caused the accident.

Judgment should be deferred by the Court of Arbitration so long as no final decision has been pronounced in the public action brought before or during the claim for compensation.

Art. XXXI.—The Court of Arbitration has the right, if it be proved by the employer or the district that the accident was due to the serious fault of the workman, to diminish or even to refuse any pension whatsoever to the sufferer or his representatives.

Art. XXXII.—When it has been proved that the accident was due to the serious fault of the head of the establishment or of one of those placed by him in charge of or to survey the works, the Court of Arbitration may increase the compensation provided under Sec. I.

The normal compensation is alone carried to the account of the district or included in its expenditure. The payment of the supplementary compensation shall be recovered from the head of the establishment.

The injured person or his representatives have full right to benefit by judicial aid for the recovery of this compensation which is guaranteed by the privilege conferred by Art. 2101 of the Civil Code, and mentioned therein under No. 6.

Art. XLIV.—The Higher Council shall draw up within six months of the promulgation of the law a list in which shall be enumerated all the industries and professions subject to its provisions. It shall set forth the series of the relative proportions of risks to which each industry or profession is liable according to the conditions under which they are carried on, which conditions should be stated in the said list.

To each class of industry at least three graduated proportions shall correspond.

The list shall be approved and made executory by decree and shall be revised every three years.

In case of omission of an industry the parties interested may apply at all times to the Minister to obtain its insertion, and it shall be added if need be to the general list by means of a decree to that effect.

Art. XLVI.—The sum to be distributed each year according to district comprises—

(1) The capital required to constitute the incomes and pensions entered on the books during the preceding year.

(2) The sums charged during the same period to the account of the district for funeral expenses, temporary compensation, and cost of administration and collection.

(3) Additional capital for a reserve fund, the amount of which shall be settled annually by the committee of management and shall not exceed one-fourth of the sum distributed during the preceding year.

Art. XLVII.—For this purpose the committee of management shall draw up every year for each parish of the district, according to notice and proposal of the

committee of sections, a list of names according to the
heads of all the establishments under the control of the
parish or commune, with particulars of their classifi-
cation, their relative proportion of risk, and if need be
the reduction of subscription allowed to each of them.

I have thought it worth while to print these
Articles, though the scheme is still under discussion, because, as compared with the German
System, the French draft bill exhibits those
gifts of expression and that lucidity of arrange-
ment which so happily characterise our agree-
able neighbours.

IV

THE NEW BILL

IT was a shrewd observation of one of the keenest critics of the Anglo-Saxon mind that ever lived, Cardinal Newman, that it takes an immense time to wind up an Englishman to the level of a dogma—that is to say, to get him to understand what a dogma is, what it involves, what it necessarily asserts, and what it unavoidably denies. Often when after great toil, with pulleys and hoists, encouragements in front and goads behind, the Englishman's bullet-head slowly appears almost on the level of the ground, something goes wrong somewhere, and down he falls to the very bottom of the pit, and the work of winding him up has to be begun all over again.

This trait of character is very noticeable in

the discussion now going on not only in Committee of the House of Commons, but in every railway shed and Directors' board room in the country about this new way of paying workmen for injuries sustained by them in the course of their employment. Nor is this surprising; for if it be difficult to get an Englishman to lay hold of a dogma at all, how much more difficult must it be to persuade him to let go an old one with which use and wont have familiarised him, and to seize upon a new one of which a month ago he had never heard,—to make him exchange his old *Mumpsimus* for a brand new *Sumpsimus.* Again and again in the course of the parliamentary discussion has this difficulty been illustrated. Again and again has the new dogma been expounded; but again and again have employers of labour and labour representatives risen in their places and started off along the very line of rail from which you thought Mr. Chamberlain had successfully shunted them half-an-hour before.

In the first two Lectures I emphasised with tiresome iteration how hitherto "in our rough island story," delinquency has been the sole basis for damages. Justice, not pity—individual wrong-doing or forbearing, not general contract of insurance—were the watchwords of our law and lawyers. It is true, as I pointed out in the first Lecture, that at an early date in our history an exception was introduced which tarnished the purity of our moral code—I mean, the doctrine which imputed to a master a negligence which was not his, but his servant's, and cast upon the employer the liability to pay damages for an act or omission of his servant which he had never authorised and had even expressly forbidden. From Lord Holt's time, and, indeed, from a much earlier date, the view has prevailed that the man who chooses to carry on his business or arrange his pleasure by means of hired labour must warrant the pecuniary capacity of his hireling to pay damages for any wrongful act or omission of the hireling done or permitted in the course of his employment. *Respondent superior* is a dogma which holds in its arms the new dogma of the new Bill.

It is worth again noting how the much-talked-of doctrine of Common Employment

was a protest against the dogma *Respondeat
superior*, and an attempt, and a very successful
attempt of our judicial legislators to restrict
the application of the dogma to persons outside the service of the same master. If my
cook scalds the butcher's boy I pay, but if she
scalds her kitchenmaid I do not pay. The
gaunt structure of society is covered with such
juridical cobwebs as this; and she, the brawny
giantess that she is, grunting and sweating
under the well-nigh intolerable burden of life,
patiently submits to be bound by them;
seldom so much as raises her head from her
toil to inquire what they are, what they
mean, however they came into existence, and
why they should be allowed to remain.

But for this remarkable exception of
Respondeat superior our old dogma was:
Nobody shall be called upon to pay for
the misfortunes of another unless those misfortunes have been directly occasioned by a
breach of that duty which each man owes his
neighbour—to take that proper amount of care
of him which according to the circumstances
of the case was his due. And in order to
ascertain what that amount of care was in

the circumstances of any particular case and whether it was lacking—let a jury be sworn.

This was the old dogma, the history of which you can read, the development of which you can trace, the consequences of which you can mark in the hundreds of volumes of our Law Reports. No branch of legal study exhibits our judges, a virile race, from Lord Holt to Lord Esher, in finer intellectual form. They toss the subject to and fro, they impale the wounded suitor upon the horns of countless dilemmas, they drive home moral obligations, they drive off illegitimate conclusions with a *verve* and a vigour as attractive and bracing as is (for the most part) the language of their judgments apt and accurate.

It is all very splendid, but, like "the pomp and circumstance of glorious war," it is expensive. It costs money and it takes time. Now Time and Money are the gods of our Israel, and hence our religious horror of litigation and our holy rage at costs.

Well am I aware of the unpopularity amongst Trades Union men of the doctrine of Common Employment; frequent have been my opportunities of observing the hardship wrought

by judges taking it upon themselves to non-
suit plaintiffs for contributory negligence ; fully
do I recognise how inapplicable to the facts
of our modern social life is the maxim *Volenti
non fit injuria*—yet certain am I of this, that
grievous though these incidents of our Common
Law are, and loudly though they call for reform,
the real enemy of the old dogma and the real
parent of the new dogma is Costs, or, as they
are called in Scotland, Expenses.

The whole country has lost its temper with
costs.   It is scandalous, the country cries, that
it should cost so much money to find out
simple facts.   Statistics are quoted to show
how it costs £14 17s. 6d. to recover £50 ; and
some stout solicitor who has made a snug
fortune out of railway companies and public
Boards and the Lands Clauses Consolidation
Act, gets up in his place in Parliament and
deplores the fact that there are in the ranks
of his profession, a few, a very few, but
still a few, practitioners, lewd fellows of the
baser sort, who are not above making costs
out of a workman's accident.   Parliament shud-
ders at such infamy, and runs amuk at costs.

Now, be it observed that if your end and

aim is to bring out the truth, to discuss the facts, to consider surrounding circumstances (and surrounding circumstances there will always be, despite the impatience of Parliament), to adjust moral claims and to fix responsibility, the process will always cost money, and if it is done properly, take time. And what is more, the process itself, call it by what new-fangled name you please, is in fact litigation. You may, though it is not easy, cheapen litigation, but its nature remains the same.

Mr. Asquith's Bill of 1893 sought to reform the Common Law and to cheapen litigation ; but as soon as it was dubbed " a Bill to enable lawyers to make costs," it was doomed. " No more costs " was the cry of an attorney-ridden world. Oh ! for some expedient to cut ourselves adrift from this living death of costs ! Then some well-informed person rose up and declared that in the remote Teutonic Fatherland there was and had been for a decade and more, a scheme in existence which had got rid once and for ever of all litigation about the origin of accidents, and consequently of all costs, and by which matters were so arranged that whenever and however an accident arose, money to

compensate it came through the post. Men
looked to Germany, and from Germany came
the new dogma.

What is it? The Bill of the Government
declares it in the first clause :—

If in any employment to which the Act applies personal
injury by accident arising out of and in the course of the
employment is caused to a workman his employer shall,
subject as hereinafter mentioned, be liable to pay
compensation in accordance with the First Schedule to
this Act.

This then is the new dogma. Consider it
for a moment before any of its beams have been
shorn by subsequent qualifications.

You have here personal liability to pay wholly
irrespective of personal delinquency. Negligence, so long the genius of this branch of
the law, is with sighing sent. Accident—
Chance takes her place. A flash of lightning
strikes a chimney-stack, properly protected by
conductors ; the chimney falls and kills a man
working at its base : the employer compensates his widow and dependents according to
scale. A workman, not known to be of intem-
perate habits, flustered with drink lights a
match in a gaseous mine and blows himself

and a score of his fellow workmen into eternity : the employer compensates the widows and children of the twenty according to scale. A workman rushing recklessly along trips and falls into a vat or pit which should have been fenced, and is gravely injured : the employer pays according to scale. A workman is engaged in dangerous works, the risks of which are fully explained to him ; he suffers an injury : the employer pays according to scale.

But if the employer instead of being guiltless is personally negligent, or acts wilfully, why then he remains liable under the provisions of that Common Law which the Bill leaves severely alone.

Repeatedly during the discussions in Committee the non-morality of the measure seemed to strike members all of a heap. Employers and Employed were heard loudly declaring that the Bill gives natural justice the lie direct.

But does it do anything of the kind ? The whole basis of the Bill is the insurance by the employer of his workmen against accidents arising out of their employment. Let us suppose that Lord Holt two hundred years ago, when a lawyer's fancy had greater scope than to-day, had declared it to be an implied term of every contract of hiring that the master guaranteed his servant against injury to life or limb whilst going about his master's business, —would not that have been a principle as capable of application and development as the law of negligence itself? Is there anything in it shocking to the moral sense? A poor man after all has but his life and his limbs, and if a fellow-mortal buys the use of the latter in the labour-market for a daily or weekly wage, is there anything contrary to natural justice in the purchaser being assumed to have ensured the said life and limbs against the happening of events, which if they do chance to happen will render the man and his belongings helpless and homeless?

It is not now a question of moral responsibility at all, but of the implied terms of an unwritten contract of hiring. It is only because we have lived so long under the bondage of moral ideas in this matter that we find it hard to be shunted suddenly on to another line of thought altogether.

I assert confidently that the principle of the

new Bill is a sound one, even although the employer who pays under it is no more a delinquent than is an insurance broker a murderer when he pays the moneys that have become due under a life-policy. It is not crime or tort, but quasi-contract.

It is, however, no easy job to take the moral law out of an Englishman's mouth. He loves to mumble it.

The Bill as introduced, and very wisely as I think, did not attempt to classify accidents, and thus avoided the possibility of any inquiry as to how the accident occurred. If it arose in the course of the workman's employment, that was to be enough; of course it must have been an accident and not an intentional act; but if an accident it were, that was to be enough.

This bold treatment of the question shocked the moral sense. The point is a small one, for the number of accidents solely attributable to the fault of the workmen is not large, but being "stuff' o' the conscience," it excited loquacity. We are all moralists in the lower branch of the Legislature, and both sides agreed that as a matter of morals the man who alone

had occasioned an accident by his serious and
wilful misconduct ought not to be allowed to
get a penny out of it. To the height of
this great argument we all arose, and I with
the rest, though remembering as I did that
in the majority of these cases the guilty
author of the accident is the first to perish by
it, thus at once escaping from the jurisdiction
of a judge of County Courts; and how too
frequently he leaves behind him in sorry
plight a widow and infant children, my
passion for punishment, my lust to indulge
my moral sentiments, was not so violent as it
seemed to be in the case of austerer persons.

Accordingly the following words were added
to the Bill : " If it is proved that the accident
is solely attributable to the serious and wilful
misconduct of a workman, any compensation
claimed in respect of injury to that workman
shall be disallowed."

Excellent morality ! But on what does it all
rest ? Upon these words, " *If it is proved.*"
That is the worst of morality : it can only
operate on facts, and facts must be proved,
and in order to prove them they must be
inquired into. You cannot say to the work-

man who holds up a bleeding stump, once his
strong right arm, " I have nothing for you."
You cannot say to a weeping widow, whose
husband lies in her back parlour a mangled
corpse, " Go, get thee to a workhouse! Your
man was a careless rogue." These gratifications
cannot be yours until the facts have been
proved, established, and declared—until our
old litigious friends, " the surrounding circumstances," have been sifted. And what is the
process by which this is done but that very
litigation the abolition of which has been
declared to be the life and soul of the whole
Bill ?

It is all very well to wag the head and say
it cannot happen—happen occasionally it must
and will. An accident occurs down a mine or
in a factory, the insurance office, which in nine
cases out of ten will have to pay, must in a
good many cases inquire into the cause of the
accident—astute persons will be employed to
look up witnesses and to take proofs—in fact,
to get up a case. True it is that the *onus*
will be on the employer, that is, the insurance
office, to show that the accident was solely
attributable to the misconduct of the work-

man, and I readily admit that in most cases
it will be very difficult to shift this *onus*; but
in those cases where it is shifted, it will become the duty of the workman or his representatives to prove that the employer was
guilty of contributory negligence, since if he
or they can establish this, the workman was
not solely to blame. Is this not, to use the
phrase employed in the House of Commons.
by Mr. Burt, to leave the door ajar and to let
in both litigation and law ?

If people could only be got to see that the
new dogma has not got a moral basis at all,
they would recognise how inexpedient it is,
even in a small number of cases, to mix up
two different systems.

If a workman acts in such a manner as to
raise the inference that he meant to make an
end of himself, so far then as he is concerned
his death or injury was no accident ; but once
the element of uncertainty enters in, it is
obviously wise to include all occurrences of
this kind, since by so doing you avoid the
necessity of proof.

However, the Bill as amended establishes
the exception I have criticised.

But for this exception, negligence (within the limits of the Bill) has disappeared, taking with her common employment, contributory negligence, and *volenti non fit injuria*. These dogmas, doctrines, maxims—call them what you will—clearly have no place in a system which exists, not for the purpose of fixing liability, but of compensating for accidents of every kind arising out of a man's employment.

I say *within the limits of the Bill*, for outside the Bill, and except so far as common employment has been cut down by the Act of 1880, these dogmas, doctrines, maxims—call them what you will—still adorn our common law and apply in all their rigour to all servants and workmen except those who are included within the Bill.

The Bill is not a measure of law reform ; indeed it is a Bill which allows the common law to remain unreformed of set purpose, and, as it were, by way of bribe to the workmen within the Bill, in order to induce them to accept the advantages it offers them, rather than to seek relief in the nonsense-ridden Courts of the land.

The Bill does not take away from the work-

man any of his common law rights or any of
his rights under the Act of 1880, but it takes
care to leave all the old lions in the path of
the man who ventures into the Queen's Courts
in pursuit of justice. It is hard to recognise
the reasonableness of this course. In all the
dangerous trades the doctrines of common
employment, contributory negligence and
assent, are abolished or rendered inapplicable ;
in the non-dangerous trades they remain in
full force.

This, then, being the new dogma, it is important to consider to whom it applies. The
Government very justly consider the Bill an
experiment, and are anxious to garner experience as to how it works in active operation
before applying it to the whole working community. The Government cannot be accused
of making the experiment on too small a scale,
for it is calculated that nearly one-half of the
whole working population are within its
scope, and the included half number all the
dangerous trades. It is easier to say who are
excluded than to enumerate the classes within
the Bill. Agricultural labourers are excluded,
except indeed so far as they may chance to be

engaged upon any work where fixed machinery
is employed; seamen and sea-apprentices are
excluded; domestic servants are excluded;
tramway-men are excluded; bargees are excluded; the building trade is excluded, except
where the building exceeds thirty feet in
height, and is being constructed, demolished
or repaired by means of scaffolding, or where
steam, water or other mechanical power is
employed. Within the Bill are railway-
men, miners, quarrymen, and men engaged
in engineering as defined by the Bill.
Factories as defined by Section 93 of the
Factory and Workshop Act, 1878, are within
the Bill; but workshops, as defined by the
same section, are not. Laundries, when worked
by steam, water or other mechanical power,
are also within the Bill.

There can be no doubt that if the Bill
becomes law, the greater number of the accidents which annually occur in our industrial
ranks will fall to be compensated under its
provisions.

The Bill provides "that the employer shall
not be liable under this Act in respect of any
injury which does not disable the workman

for a period of at least *two weeks* from earning
full wages at the work at which he was
employed."

You will remember that by the German
scheme the injured workman did not become
chargeable upon the corporation of employers
until he had been in bed thirteen weeks; but
by this Bill the English workman must be
compensated by the individual employer at
the end of a fortnight.

The German system fosters and maintains
as one of its two integral parts a great friendly
society or group of affiliated societies maintained as to two-thirds of their total sub-
scriptions entirely by the working people, and
casts on these funds the duty of maintaining
the injured workman for thirteen weeks. The
English Bill leaves the first fortnight of illness
unprovided for, and then makes the individual
employer responsible for what the German
group of employers is not responsible for—
another eleven weeks.

It is much disputed what will be the effect
of the Bill if it becomes law on our great
friendly societies. Some say it will most
injuriously affect them; for workmen will not,

so it is suggested, subscribe to a society when
they will have a right to compensation, according to a liberal scale, from their employer in
case of accidents; and accidents, it is pointed
out, are the chief causes of a workman's illness.
To this it is replied—*first*, there is a fortnight
left unprovided for; *second*, there is a chance
of the employer being unable to pay the compensation awarded; and *third*, friendly societies have other objects besides compensation
for accidents. There is sickness arising from
ill-health, and there is old age as well as other
objects upon which the funds liberated by the
operation of the Bill may well and easily
be spent. The point is not one to dogmatise
upon, but the destruction of our huge friendly
societies cannot be contemplated without
dismay; and I therefore rejoice to observe
that the best-instructed opinion is that they
will not be injured by the Bill, though some
of them may require a little readjustment.
Societies which are purely accident societies,
as, for example, the schemes that have been
established by some of the railway companies
for providing the necessary funds to compensate for accidents, are in greater peril, and

in most instances will, I expect, abruptly
terminate.

I have already referred to another great
difference between the German and proposed
British system. In the former the liability to
pay compensation is a trade liability and is
borne by the whole trade; but in the latter it
is an individual liability. By the Bill the
employer is liable just in the same way as he
is liable at common law for his own negligence,
and as he is, under the Act of 1880, for the
negligence in certain cases, of his servants.

This is indeed a difference.

I confess, as a lawyer, the British proposal
is the easier of comprehension, since it may
be based upon an implied obligation of the
employer to insure his workman's life and
limbs against accident whilst the workman is
in his employ. But that there should be
solidarity amongst employers is more a religious than a legal idea. It has its advantages, but it seems a very illogical half-way
house between individual and State responsibility.

Of course it is an excellent thing for the
workman, since it guarantees him the price of

his wounds as per scale. What an injured
man wants is not a judgment debt or a right
to prove in bankruptcy, but cash. In Germany
he gets his cash, in Austria he gets his cash,
by the French scheme he would get his cash,
by the British scheme he will frequently lose
it. This is thought very hard. Poor fellow!
why should he not be paid? But who is to
pay him? He can only be paid by, the employer, by the trade, or by the community.
Why should the community pay him any more
than it pays the man who is struck by lightning or gored by a bull? Why should one
colliery proprietor pay for the accidents that
occur down the pits of another colliery proprietor? It is hard to say, whereas it is not
difficult to find a reason for making the
individual employer pay if he can. Of course
if he cannot pay it is hard upon the workman
as it is upon all the employer's creditors. It is
said nobody need have given him credit,
whereas the poor working man was bound to
work for him. This reasoning may be pushed
too far. Life presses heavily upon other folk
as well as on the artisan.

At any rate the Bill does not make the

plight of the working man worse than before. At common law his employer is the only person he can shoot at. By this Bill he can shoot at him more frequently. If the employer goes bankrupt he only does what he could have done before.

At the same time it is impossible not to notice a growing disposition to treat accidents happening in industrial life as a class by themselves, against which there ought to be compulsory insurance. This Bill does not make insurance compulsory, though it is so framed as to make it almost necessary. The public seem already to expect that the compensation provided for by the Bill is always to be forthcoming, and it can hardly be doubted that if experience was to prove that in many cases the working man did not in practice get his scale-charges for accidents a demand would be made for national insurance.

The scale of compensation provided for by the Bill will be found in the First Schedule, and it is so simple in its character as to need no explanation. (See Appendix A.)

The scale is a liberal one, and, on the whole, is as good as the award of a jury would be,

tempered as such awards are by the discretion
of judges and the wisdom of counsel not caring
to risk a new trial. Discussion has arisen as
to who ought to be dependants under Sec. 5,
whether, for example, an able-bodied father
can properly be dependent upon the earnings
of a child, but such questions may safely be
left to the discretion of the arbitrator. The
12th Section of the First Schedule also excited
opposition, but this much may certainly be
said for it, that it is in the interest of the working man to be paid off as speedily as possible,
since he thereby is rid of the risk of the future
insolvency or incapacity of the employer to
make the weekly payments.

The Second Schedule arranges the manner
in which applications for compensation under
the Bill are to be dealt with.

Here we get upon the vexed question of
procedure. The mode proposed is Arbitration.
The Bill contemplates the existence of a Committee representative of an employer and his
workmen having power to settle matters under
the Act; and by this Committee, or by their
Arbitrator, settled the matter will be unless
either party objects.

In case of objection or if there be no such
Committee, the matters are to be settled by a
single arbitrator or Conciliation Board to be
agreed upon between the parties, or, in the
absence of agreement, by the County Court
Judge, unless the Lord Chancellor thinks it
inconvenient that the County Court Judge
should be called upon to act, and if this be
so the arbitrator is to be appointed by such
County Court Judge.

Of course it is obvious that instances can
and must arise more or less of a litigious character; for example, one question which will
frequently arise will be whether the injury was
caused by an accident arising out of and in
the course of the employment of the workman
who was injured. In other words, where and
when was the admitted injury sustained? Another question which may arise is, whether the
injury was caused by the personal negligence
or wilful act of the employer, or of any person
for whose act or default the employer is responsible. If the injury was so caused the
employer remains liable at Common Law, and
possibly under the Act of 1880; and in this case
the arbitrator can have no authority, except

by the agreement of the parties. A third question which may frequently arise is, whether the employment is one to which the Act applies. A fourth is whether the accident was solely attributable to the serious and wilful misconduct of the workman. All these are questions which may have to be dealt with by the arbitrator, and his award upon them is final.

The provisions as to notice are, that notice of the accident shall be given as soon as practicable after the happening thereof, and that the claim for compensation shall be made within six months from the occurrence of the accident, or, in case of death, within twelve months from the time of death, subject however to the proviso that the want of such notice shall not be a bar to the maintenance of such proceedings if it is found in the proceedings for settling the claim that the employer is not prejudiced in his defence by the absence of such notice, or that such notice was occasioned by accident or other reasonable cause.

In their furious zeal against Costs, the

House of Commons has provided that in no
proceedings under the Bill shall Counsel or
Solicitor be allowed to appear, except by
special leave, or on appeal to the Court of
Appeal, nor shall any Solicitor have a lien on
the compensation moneys for his costs. Cromwell once found to his disgust in his raid
against the Court of Chancery that the "sons
of Zeruiah" were too much for him. I hope
Mr. Chamberlain may succeed where Cromwell
failed.

The question of contracting out, around
which so fierce a battle was fought in 1893, is,
having regard to the provisions of this Bill,
almost without importance, since contracting
out is expressly forbidden except in circumstances not likely to be of frequent
occurrence.

Those circumstances will be found stated in
the 4th Sub-section of Clause I.

The effect of this is that the employer cannot contract himself out of the Bill except by
a certified scheme not less favourable to the
workmen and their dependants than the provisions of the Bill itself.

A valuable clause, relating to sub-contracts, will also be found in the Bill (Clause 2).

I do not think I can usefully add any more by way of explanation of a measure which has not yet passed through the crucible of the House of Lords.

APPENDIX A

A BILL

[AS AMENDED IN COMMITTEE]

TO

Amend the Law with respect to Compensation to Workmen for accidental Injuries suffered in the course of their Employment.   A.D. 1897.

Be it enacted by the Queen's most Excellent Majesty, by and with the advice and consent of the Lords Spiritual and Temporal, and Commons, in this present Parliament assembled, and by the authority of the
5 same, as follows :—

1.—(1.) If in any employment to which this Act Liability applies, personal injury by accident arising out of and of certain in the course of the employment is caused to a work-employers man, his employer shall, subject as herein-after men-men for
10 tioned, be liable to pay compensation in accordance injuries. with the First Schedule to this Act, such compensation shall be payable whether the injury occasioned arises from the act of the employer or of some person in his employ, or from the act of a stranger thereto.   Pro-

vided that where such injury shall be occasioned by the act of a stranger under circumstances creating a legal liability to pay damages in respect thereof, the workman may at his option proceed either at law against such person to recover damages or against his employer 5 for compensation under this Act, and if he be compensated under this Act, the employer shall be entitled to enforce in the name of the workman all rights of action possessed by him against the person occasioning such injury as aforesaid. 10

(2.) Provided that :—

(*a.*) The employer shall not be liable under this Act in respect of any injury which does not disable the workman for a period of at least two weeks from earning full wages at the work at which 15 he was employed ;

(*b.*) When it is decided, as hereafter provided, that the injury was caused by the personal negligence or wilful act of the employer or of some person for whose act or default the employer is respon- 20 sible, nothing in this Act shall affect any civil liability of the employer, but in that case the amount of damages due from such employer may, at the request of the persons claiming compensation, be settled by arbitration in ac- 25 cordance with the Second Schedule to this Act, or may at the option of such persons be recovered from such employer by the same proceedings as were open to such persons before the commencement of this Act; but the em- 30 ployer shall not be liable to pay compensation both independently of and also under this Act, and shall not be liable to pay compensation independently of this act, except in case of such personal negligence or wilful act : 35

A.D. 1897.

(c.) If it is proved that the accident is solely attributable to the serious and wilful misconduct of a workman, any compensation claimed in respect of injury to that workman shall be disallowed.

(3.) If any question arises as to whether the injury was caused by the personal negligence or wilful act of the employer, or of any person for whose act or default the employer is responsible, or whether the injury was caused by accident arising out of and in the course of the employment of the workman injured, or whether the accident was solely attributable to the serious and wilful misconduct of the workman in respect of whose injuries compensation is claimed, or as to the amount or duration of compensation under this Act, or otherwise as to the liability for compensation under this Act, the question, if not settled by agreement, and any question as to whether the employment is one to which this Act applies, shall, subject to the provisions of the First Schedule to this Act, be settled by arbitration, in accordance with the second Schedule to this Act. Proceedings for the recovery under this Act of compensation for an injury shall not be maintainable unless notice of the accident has been given as soon as practicable after the happening thereof, and the claim for compensation with respect to such accident has been made within six months from the occurrence of the accident causing the injury, or, in case of death, within twelve months from the time of death. Provided always that the want of such notice shall not be a bar to the maintenance of such proceedings if it is found in the proceedings for settling the claim that the employer is not prejudiced in his defence by the absence of such notice, or that such absence was occasioned by mistake or other reasonable cause. Notices shall be served in

A.D. 1897. the manner provided for by the Employers' Liability
Act, 1880, section seven.

(4.) If the Registrar of Friendly Societies, after
ascertaining the views of the employers and workmen,
certifies that any scheme of compensation or insurance 5
for the workmen in any employment is on the whole
not less favourable to the workmen and their dependants than the provisions of this Act, the employer may,
until the certificate is revoked, contract with any of
those workmen that the provisions of the scheme shall be 10
substituted for the provisions of this Act, and thereupon
the employer shall be liable only in accordance with the
scheme, but, save as aforesaid, this Act shall apply,
notwithstanding any contract to the contrary made
after the commencement of this Act. No scheme shall 15
be so certified which contains an obligation upon the
workmen to join the scheme as a condition of their
hiring.

If the funds under any such scheme are not sufficient
to meet the compensation payable thereout the em- 20
ployer shall be liable to make good the amount of compensation which would be payable under this Act.

(5.) The Registrar of Friendly Societies shall in
every year make a report of his proceedings under
this Act, and that report shall be laid before Parlia- 25
ment.

(6.) If any workmen or their representatives shall
submit to the said Registrar primâ facie evidence that
the provisions of any scheme are no longer so favourable to the workman as the provisions of this Act, or that 30
the provisions of such scheme are being violated, or that
the same is not being fairly administered by the employers, or that satisfactory reasons exist for revoking
the certificate, then he shall examine into the complaint,
and if satisfied that good cause exists for such com- 35

plaint, shall, unless the cause of complaint is removed, A.D. 1897. revoke the certificate.

(7.) Whenever a scheme has been certified as aforesaid, it shall be the duty of the employer to answer all inquiries and to furnish all such accounts as may from time to time be required by the Registrar of Friendly Societies.

2. Where any person in the execution of any work within the scope of his trade or business, and for the purpose of executing such work, is in occupation of or has control over the place or premises in or upon which such work is to be done, he shall be liable to any workman engaged in the execution of the work therein or thereupon for the amount of any claim which such workman may have under this Act, or in respect of personal negligence or wilful act independently of this Act, against any sub-contractor. Provided that any person liable under this section shall be entitled to indemnity against any other person who would have been liable independently of this section. All questions arising under this section shall be settled by arbitration as provided by this Act.

Sub-contracting.

3. Where an employer who is the owner or occupier of any premises has engaged or contracted with any other person to execute any work, act, or thing in, upon, or about such premises not within the scope of the trade or business of such employer, and such other person employs or directs and controls the workmen engaged in such work, act, or thing, then, in the event of any of such workmen being injured whilst so engaged, such other person shall be deemed to be the employer of such workmen for the purposes of this Act, and not the owner or occupier of the premises.

Liability of contractor for extraneous work.

4. Where any employer becomes liable under this Act to pay compensation to any workman or his representatives in respect of any accident, and is entitled to any sum from insurers of such liability, then in the event of the bankruptcy or liquidation of such employer such work-

Compensation to workmen in case of bankruptcy of employer.

A.D. 1897. man or representative shall have a charge upon the sum aforesaid for the payment of the money so due to him.

Application of Act and definitions. 5.—(1.) This Act shall apply only to employment on, in, or about a railway, factory, mine, quarry, or engineering work, and to employment on, in, or about any building exceeding thirty feet in height, which is being constructed, demolished, or repaired by means of a scaffolding, or on which machinery driven by steam, water, or other mechanical power is being used for the purpose of the construction, demolition, or repair thereof.

(2.) In this Act—

"Railway" means the railway of any railway company to which the Regulation of Railways Act, 1873, applies, and "railway" and "railway company" have the same meaning as in that Act, and includes light railways made under the Light Railways Act, 1896.

36 & 37 Vict. c. 48. s. 2.

"Factory" has the same meaning as in the Factory and Workshop Acts, 1878 to 1891, and also includes any dock, wharf, quay, warehouse, machinery, or plant, to which any provision of the Factory Acts is applied by the Factory and Workshop Act, 1895, and every laundry worked by steam, water, or other mechanical power.

41 & 42 Vict. c. 16. s. 93, 54 & 55 Vict. c. 75.

"Mine" means a mine to which the Coal Mines Regulation Act, 1887, or the Metalliferous Mines Regulation Act, 1872, applies.

58 & 59 Vict. c. 37. s. 23. 50 & 51 Vict. c. 58. ss. 3, 75. 35 & 36 Vict. c. 77. ss. 3, 41. 57 & 58 Vict. c. 42.

"Quarry" means a quarry under the Quarries Act, 1894.

"Engineering work" means any work of construction or alteration of a railroad, harbour, dock, canal, or sewer, and includes any other work on which machinery driven by steam, water,

or other mechanical power is used for the A.D. 1897.
purpose of the construction or alteration
thereof.

" Employer " includes any body of persons corporate
or unincorporate.

" Workman " includes every person who is engaged
in an employment to which this Act applies,
whether by way of manual labour or otherwise, and whether his agreement is one of
service or apprenticeship or otherwise, and is
expressed or implied, is oral or in writing.

6.—(1.) This Act shall not apply to persons in the Applica-
naval or military service of the Crown, but otherwise tion to
shall apply to any employment by or under the Crown workmen
in employ-
to which this Act would apply if the employer were a ment of
private person. Crown.

(2.) The Treasury may, by warrant laid before Parliament, modify for the purposes of this Act their
warrant made under section one of the Superannuation 50 & 51
Act, 1887. Vict. c. 67.

7. Any contract existing at the commencement of Provision
this Act, whereby a workman relinquishes any right to as to
existing
compensation from the employer for personal injury contracts.
arising out of and in the course of his employment, shall
not, for the purposes of this Act, be deemed to continue
after the time at which the workman's contract of
service would determine if notice of the determina-
tion thereof were given at the commencement of this
Act.

8.—(1.) This act shall come into operation on the Com-
thirty-first day of March one thousand eight hundred mence-
ment of
and ninety-eight. Act and

(2.) This Act may be cited as the Workmen's Com- short title.
pensation Act, 1897.

SCHEDULES.

FIRST SCHEDULE

SCALE AND CONDITIONS OF COMPENSATION.

Scale.

(1.) The amount of compensation under this Act 5
shall be—

(*a.*) where death results from the injury—

(i.) if the workman leaves dependants, a sum
equal to his earnings during the three years
next preceding the injury, or the sum of one 10
hundred and fifty pounds, whichever of those
sums is the larger, but not exceeding in any
case three hundred pounds, provided that the
amount of any weekly payments made under
this Act shall be deducted from such sum ; and 15

(ii.) if he leaves no dependants, the reasonable
expenses of his medical attendance and burial.
not exceeding ten pounds ;

(*b*) in case of total or partial incapacity for work
resulting from the injury, a weekly payment during 20
the incapacity after the second week not exceeding
fifty per cent. of his average weekly earnings at
that employment during the previous twelve months.
but if the period of his engagement has been less
than twelve months, then the average during the 25
period of his actual engagement, such weekly payment not to exceed one pound.

(2.) In fixing the amount of the weekly payment, A.D. 1897. regard shall be had to the difference between the amount of the weekly earnings of the workman before the accident and the amount which he is able to earn after 5 the accident.

(3.) The payment shall be made on the application of the person entitled thereto, or his authorised representatives.

(4.) The payment shall, in case of death, be made to 10 the legal personal representative of the workman, or, if he has no legal personal representative, to his dependants, or, if he leaves no dependants, to the person to whom the expenses are due.

(5.) The expression "dependants" in this schedule 9 & 10 15 means such members of the workman's family specified Vict. c. 93. in the Fatal Accidents Act, 1846, as were wholly or in part dependent upon the earnings of the workman at the time of or immediately prior to his death ; and any question as to who is a dependant, or as to the amount 20 payable to each dependant shall, in default of agreement, be settled by arbitration under this Act.

(6.) The sum allotted as compensation may be invested or otherwise applied for his benefit as directed by the committee or other arbitrator.

25 (7.) Any sum ordered by the committee or arbitrator to be invested may be ordered to be invested in whole or in part in the Post Office Savings Bank by the registrar of the county court in his name as registrar.

(8.) Any sum so ordered to be invested may be 30 accepted by the Postmaster-General as a deposit in the name of the registrar as such, and the provisions of any statute or regulations respecting the limits of deposits in savings bank, and the declaration to be made by a depositor, shall not apply to such sums.

35 (9.) No part of any money invested in the name of

A.D. 1897. the registrar of any county court in the Post Office
Savings Bank under this Act, shall be paid out to any
registrar, except upon authority addressed to the Postmaster-General by the Treasury or by the judge.

(10.) Any person deriving any benefit under any 5
moneys paid into a post office savings bank under the
provisions of this Act, may nevertheless open an account
in a post office savings bank or in any other savings
bank in his own name, without being liable to any
penalties imposed by any statute or regulations in re- 10
spect of the opening of accounts in two savings banks,
or of two accounts in the same savings bank.

(11.) Any weekly payment may be reviewed at the
request either of the employer or of the workman, and
on such review may be ended, diminished or increased, 15
subject to the maximum above provided, and the amount
of payment shall, in default of agreement, be settled by
arbitration under this Act.

(12.) Where any weekly payment has been continued
for not less than twelve months the liability thereof 20
may, on the application of either the workman or the
employer, be redeemed by the payment of a lump sum,
to be settled by arbitration under this Act, but not
exceeding three hundred and twelve times the weekly
payment payable at the date of the application.   25

(13.) A weekly payment shall not be capable of being
assigned, charged, or attached, and shall not pass to any
other person by operation of law.

(14.) In the application of the Act and of this
schedule to Scotland the expression "dependants," 30
means the persons who according to the law of Scotland
are entitled to sue the employer for damages or solatium
in respect of the death of the workman, and who are
wholly or in part dependant upon the earnings of the
workman at the time of or immediately prior to his death. 35

SECOND SCHEDULE.

ARBITRATION.

The following provisions shall apply for settling any
matter which under this Act is to be settled by arbi-
5 tration :—

(1.) If any committee, representative of an employer
and his workmen, exists with power to settle matters
under this Act in the case of the employer and workmen, the matter shall, unless either party object, by
10 notice in writing sent to the other party before the
committee meet to consider the matter, be settled by
the arbitration of such committee, or be referred by
them in their discretion to an arbitrator.

(2.) If either party so objects, or there is no such
15 committee, the matter shall be settled by a single arbitrator or conciliation board agreed on by the parties, or
in the absence of agreement by the county court judge,
or if in England the Lord Chancellor certifies that
under the circumstances of that particular district it is
20 not convenient that the county court judge should be
called upon to act as arbitrator, by a single arbitrator
appointed by such county court judge.

(3.) In cases in which the county court judge or an
arbitrator appointed by him is the arbitrator, the work-
25 man or his representative may deliver to the registrar
of the county court of the district in which he resides
a statement of the nature of his claim, with his name
and address and that of the employer, and it shall be
the duty of the registrar to give notice of the said
30 claim to the employer, and to make the necessary

I

A.D.1897. arrangements for the arbitration, and give notice thereof to both parties, and all such claims may be amended by the arbitrator on such terms as to adjournment or otherwise as he thinks just, in order that the questions in dispute may be disposed of. 5

(4.) Any arbitrator other than the county court judge shall be paid out of moneys to be provided by Parliament in accordance with regulations to be made by the Treasury.

(5.) The Arbitration Act, 1889, shall not apply to 10 any arbitration under this Act, but an arbitrator may, if he thinks fit, submit any question of law for the decision of the county court judge, and the decision of the judge on any question of law, either on such submission, or in any case where he himself acts as arbitrator under this 15 Act, shall, subject to a right of appeal in every such case by any party to Her Majesty's Court of Appeal, be final ; and the county court judge, or the arbitrator appointed by him, shall, when sitting as arbitrator, have the same powers of procuring the attendance of 20 witnesses and the production of documents as if the claim for compensation had been made by plaint in the county court.

(6.) In any proceedings under this Act no party or other person shall appear to be attended by counsel 25 or solicitor except by the leave of the court or arbitrator, or on any appeal to the Court of Appeal.

(7.) The costs of the arbitration shall be in the discretion of the arbitrator.

(8.) Where the amount of compensation under this 30 Act shall have been ascertained, or any weekly payment varied, or any other matter decided, under this Act, either by a committee or by an arbitrator or by agreement, a memorandum thereof shall be sent by the said committee or arbitrator, or by any party interested, 35

to the registrar of the county court for the district in A.D. 1897.
which any person entitled to such compensation resides,
who shall, on being satisfied as to its genuineness,
record such memorandum in a special register without
5 charge, and thereupon the said memorandum shall for
all purposes be enforceable as a county court judgment.
Provided that the county court judge may at any time
rectify such register.

(9.) The duty of a county court judge under this
10 Act shall, subject to rules of court, be part of the
duties of the county court, and the officers of the court
shall act accordingly.

(10.) Any sum awarded as compensation shall be
paid on the receipt of the person entitled, and his
15 solicitor or agent shall not be entitled to recover from
him, or to claim a lien on the amount recovered for,
any costs except such as have been awarded by the
arbitrator.

(11.) The Secretary of State at the request of any
20 committee, judge, or other arbitrator shall appoint
legally qualified medical practitioner to report on any
matter which seems material to any question arising in
the arbitration, and the expense of any such medical
practitioner, shall, subject to treasury regulations, be
25 paid out of moneys to be provided by Parliament.

(12.) In the application of this schedule to Scotland
" sheriff " shall be substituted for " county court judge,"
" sheriff court " for " county court," and " act of sede-
runt " for " rules of court." Any award or agreement
30 as to compensation under this Act may be recorded in
the books of council and session or sheriff court books,
and shall be enforceable in like manner as a recorded
decree arbitral. Any application to the sheriff as
arbitrator shall be heard, tried, and determined sum-
35 marily in the manner provided by the fifty-second

section of the Sheriff Courts (Scotland) Act, 1876, subject to the declaration that it shall be competent to either party to require the sheriff to state a case on any question of law determined by him, and his decision thereon in such case may be submitted to either division of the Court of Session, who, if they consider that the point involved is of general importance, may hear and determine the same finally, and remit to the sheriff with instruction as to the judgment to be pronounced.

(13.) In the application of this schedule to Ireland the expression "county court judge" shall include the recorder of any city or town.

APPENDIX B

CHAPTER 42

*An Act to extend and regulate the Liability of A.D. 1880
Employers to make Compensation for Personal
Injuries suffered by Workmen in their service.*
[7th September, 1880.]

BE it enacted by the Queen's most Excellent Majesty,
by and with the advice and consent of the Lords
Spiritual and Temporal, and Commons, in this present
Parliament assembled, and by the authority of the same,
as follows:

1. Where [after the commencement of this Act] Amend-
personal injury is caused to a workman ment of law.

 (1.) By reason of any defect in the condition of the
   ways, works, machinery, or plant connected
   with or used in the business of the employer; or

 (2.) By reason of the negligence of any person in the
   service of the employer who has any superintendence entrusted to him whilst in the exercise
   of such superintendence; or

¹ Words within brackets repealed by Statute Law Revision
Act of 1894.

(3.) By reason of the negligence of any person in the service of the employer to whose orders or directions the workman at the time of the injury was bound to conform, and did conform, where such injury resulted from his having so conformed; or

(4.) By reason of the act or omission of any person in the service of the employer done or made in obedience to the rules or byelaws of the employer, or in obedience to particular instructions given by any person delegated with the authority of the employer in that behalf; or

(5.) By reason of the negligence of any person in the service of the employer who has the charge or control of any signal, points, locomotive engine, or train upon a railway,

the workman, or in case the injury results in death, the legal personal representatives of the workman, and any persons entitled in case of death, shall have the same right of compensation and remedies against the employer as if the workman had not been a workman of nor in the service of the employer, nor engaged in his work.

Exceptions to amendment of law.

2. A workman shall not be entitled under this Act to any right of compensation or remedy against the employer in any of the following cases; that is to say,

(1.) Under sub-section one of section one, unless the defect therein mentioned arose from, or had not been discovered or remedied owing to the negligence of the employer, or of some person in the service of the employer, and entrusted by him with the duty of seeing that the ways, works, machinery, or plant were in proper condition.

(2.) Under sub-section four of section one, unless the A.D. 1880. injury resulted from some impropriety or defect in the rules, byelaws, or instructions therein mentioned; provided that where a rule or byelaw has been approved or has been accepted as a proper rule or byelaw by one of Her Majesty's Principal Secretaries of State, or by the Board of Trade or any other department of the Government, under or by virtue of any Act of Parliament, it shall not be deemed for the purposes of this Act to be an improper or defective rule or byelaw.

(3.) In any case where the workman knew of the defect or negligence which caused the injury, and failed within a reasonable time to give, or cause to be given, information thereof to the employer or some person superior to himself in the service of the employer, unless he was aware that the employer or such superior already knew of the said defect or negligence.

3. The amount of compensation recoverable under this Act shall not exceed such sum as may be found to be equivalent to the estimated earnings, during the three years preceding the injury, of a person in the same grade employed during those years in the like employment and in the district in which the workman is employed at the time of the injury.

Limit of sum recoverable as compensation.

4. An action for the recovery under this Act of compensation for an injury shall not be maintainable unless notice that injury has been sustained is given within six weeks, and the action is commenced within six months from the occurrence of the accident causing the injury, or, in case of death, within twelve months

Limit of time for recovery of compensation.

A.D. 1880. from the time of death : Provided always, that in case of death the want of such notice shall be no bar to the maintenance of such action if the judge shall be of opinion that there was reasonable excuse for such want of notice.

Money payable under penalty to be deducted from compensation under Act.

5. There shall be deducted from any compensation awarded to any workman, or representatives of a workman, or persons claiming by, under, or through a workman in respect of any cause of action arising under this Act, any penalty or part of a penalty which may have been paid in pursuance of any other Act of Parliament to such workman, representatives, or persons in respect of the same cause of action ; and where an action has been brought under this Act by any workman, or the representatives of any workman, or any persons claiming by, under, or through such workman for compensation in respect of any cause of action arising under this Act, and payment has not previously been made of any penalty or part of a penalty under any other Act of Parliament in respect of the same cause of action, such workman, representatives, or person shall not be entitled thereafter to receive any penalty or part of a penalty under any other Act of Parliament in respect of the same cause of action.

Trial of actions.

6.—(1.) Every action for recovery of compensation under this Act shall be brought in a county court, but may, upon the application of either plaintiff or defendant, be removed into a superior court in like manner and upon the same conditions as an action commenced in a county court may by law be removed.

(2.) Upon the trial of any such action in a county court before the judge without a jury one or more assessors may be appointed for the purpose of ascertaining the amount of compensation.

(3.) For the purpose of regulating the conditions and mode of appointment and remuneration of such assessors, and all matters of procedure relating to their duties, and also for the purpose of consolidating any actions under this Act in a county court, and otherwise preventing multiplicity of such actions, rules and regulations may be made, varied, and repealed from time to time in the same manner as rules and regulations for regulating the practice and procedure in other actions in county courts.

"County court" shall, with respect to Scotland, mean the "Sheriff's Court," and shall, with respect to Ireland, mean the "Civil Bill Court."

In Scotland any action under this Act may be re- moved to the Court of Session at the instance of either party, in the manner provided by, and subject to the conditions prescribed by, section nine of the Sheriff Courts (Scotland) Act, 1877.

In Scotland the sheriff may conjoin actions arising out of the same occurrence or cause of action, though at the instance of different parties and in respect of different injuries.

7. Notice in respect of an injury under this Act shall give the name and address of the person injured, and shall state in ordinary language the cause of the injury and the date at which it was sustained, and shall be served on the employer, or, if there is more than one employer, upon one of such employers.

The notice may be served by delivering the same to or at the residence or place of business of the person on whom it is to be served.

The notice may also be served by post by a registered letter addressed to the person on whom it is to be served at his last known place of residence or place of business; and, if served by post, shall be deemed to have been served at the time when a letter containing the same would be delivered in the ordinary course of post; and, in proving the service of such notice, it shall be sufficient to prove that the notice was properly addressed and registered.

Where the employer is a body of persons corporate or unincorporate, the notice shall be served by delivering the same at or by sending it by post in a registered letter addressed to the office, or, if there be more than one office, any one of the offices of such body.

A notice under this section shall not be deemed invalid by reason of any defect or inaccuracy therein, unless the judge who tries the action arising from the injury mentioned in the notice shall be of opinion that the defendant in the action is prejudiced in his defence by such defect or inaccuracy, and that the defect or inaccuracy was for the purpose of misleading.

Definitions.

8. For the purposes of this Act, unless the context otherwise requires,—

The expression "person who has superintendence entrusted to him" means a person whose sole or principal duty is that of superintendence, and who is not ordinarily engaged in manual labour:

The expression "employer" includes a body of persons corporate or unincorporate:

38 & 39 Vict. c. 90.

The expression "workman" means railway servant and any person to whom the Employers and Workmen Act, 1875, applies.

Commencement of Act.

9. [Repealed, Statute Law Revision Act, 1894.]

Short title.

10. This Act may be cited as the Employers' Liability Act, 1880, and shall continue in force till the thirty-first day of December one thousand eight hundred

and eighty-seven, and to the end of the then next Session
of Parliament, and no longer, unless Parliament shall
otherwise determine, and all actions commenced under
this Act before that period shall be continued as if the
said Act had not expired.[1]

[1] This Act was continued until 31st December, 1889, by 51-52
Vict., c. 58, and has since that date been annually included in
the Expiring Laws Continuance Acts.

AN OUTLINE OF THE LAW OF LIBEL.

Six Lectures delivered in the Middle Temple Hall during
Michaelmas Term, 1896.

By W. BLAKE ODGERS, of the Middle Temple, M.A.,
LL.D., Q.C., Author of a " Digest of the Law of Libel
and Slander." Globe 8vo, 3s. 6d.

PALL MALL GAZETTE.—" It is a very good book indeed
. . . He gives a very fluent, even entertaining abridgment of his
subject, such as only a master of it, as he has proved himself in his
larger work, could make."

DAILY CHRONICLE.—"Few branches of the law are so
amusing as the law of libel, and Dr. Blake Odgers, who is the
highest authority upon the solemn side of the subject, has done the
world a real service in publishing his admirable lectures. . . . The
little book is indeed so full of good things that it is quite impossible to do justice to it. . . . deserves a wide and popular circu-
lation."

WESTMINSTER GAZETTE.—"There is a great deal in this
little book which everyone might know and remember with profit
to themselves."

DAILY MAIL.—" Is in all respects excellent, and since every
man and woman is liable at some time or other to be mixed up in a
libel case, it would be well that this admirable treatise on a tender
subject should be widely bought and assiduously studied."

MANCHESTER GUARDIAN.—" These lectures are a model of
what such lectures should be ; they are exceedingly interesting, the
name of their author is itself a guarantee of accuracy, and they are
as full and comprehensive as the occasion permitted."

MACMILLAN AND CO., LTD., LONDON.

2

MACMILLAN AND CO.'S BOOKS ON LAW.

THE STUDENT'S GUIDE TO THE BAR. Sixth Edition.
Revised and edited by JOHN P. BATE, of Lincoln's Inn, Barrister-at-Law,
Lecturer in Law at Trinity Hall, Cambridge. Crown 8vo, 2s. 6d. net.

THE PRINCIPLES OF INTERNATIONAL LAW. By T. J.
LAWRENCE, M.A., LL.D. Crown 8vo, 12s. 6d. net.

INTERNATIONAL LAW AND INTERNATIONAL RE-
LATIONS. An attempt to ascertain the best method of discussing the
topics of international law. By J. K. STEPHEN, B.A., of the Inner
Temple, Barrister-at-Law. Crown 8vo, 6s.

COMMERCIAL LAW. An Elementary Text-Book for Commercial
Classes. By J. E. C. MUNRO, LL.M., of the Middle Temple, Barrister-at-
Law. Globe 8vo, 3s. 6d. [*Commercial Class-Books.*

By Sir JAMES FITZJAMES STEPHEN, Bart., K.C.S.I., D.C.L.

A HISTORY OF THE CRIMINAL LAW OF ENGLAND.
In Three Vols. 8vo, 48s.

A GENERAL VIEW OF THE CRIMINAL LAW OF ENGLAND.
Second Edition. 8vo, 14s.

A DIGEST OF THE LAWS OF EVIDENCE. Sixth Edition.
Crown 8vo, 6s.

A DIGEST OF THE CRIMINAL LAW (Crimes and Punishments).
Edited by HARRY L. STEPHEN, Barrister-at-Law. Fifth Edition, revised.
8vo, 16s.

A DIGEST OF THE LAW OF CRIMINAL PROCEDURE IN
INDICTABLE OFFENCES. By Sir JAMES FITZJAMES STEPHEN, Bart.,
K.C.S.I., D.C.L., formerly a Judge of the High Court of Justice, Queen's
Bench Division, and HERBERT STEPHEN, Esq., LL.M., of the Inner
Temple, Barrister-at-Law. 8vo, 12s. 6d.

A HANDY BOOK OF THE LABOUR LAWS. Being a Popular
Guide to the Employers' and Workmen Act 1875, Trade Union Acts
1871, 1876, and 1893, &c. With Introductions, Notes, and the Authorised
Rules and Forms for the use of workmen. Third Edition, revised. Crown
8vo, 3s. 6d. net.

ADOPTION AND AMENDMENT OF CONSTITUTIONS IN
EUROPE AND AMERICA. By CHARLES BORGEAUD, awarded the Rossi
Prize by the Law Faculty of Paris. Translated by Professor C. D. HAZEN.
With an Introduction by JOHN M. VINCENT. Crown 8vo, 8s. 6d. net.

SOURCES OF THE CONSTITUTION OF THE UNITED
STATES, CONSIDERED IN RELATION TO COLONIAL AND ENGLISH
HISTORY. By C. ELLIS STEVENS, LL.D., D.C.L., F.S.A. (Edinburgh).
Crown 8vo, 6s. 6d. net.

MUNICIPAL HOME RULE. A Study in Administration. By
Professor FRANK J. GOODNOW, A.M., LL.B. Crown 8vo, 6s. 6d. net.

MACMILLAN AND CO., LTD., LONDON.

MACMILLAN AND CO.'S BOOKS ON LAW.

THE ENGLISH CITIZEN SERIES.

HIS RIGHTS AND RESPONSIBILITIES.

Edited by Sir HENRY CRAIK, K.C.B.

Crown 8vo, 2s. 6d. each.

CENTRAL GOVERNMENT. By H. D. TRAILL.
THE ELECTORATE AND THE LEGISLATURE. By SPENCER WALPOLE.
THE LAND LAWS. By Sir F. POLLOCK, Bart.
THE PUNISHMENT AND PREVENTION OF CRIME. By Col. Sir EDMUND DU CANE.
LOCAL GOVERNMENT. By M. D. CHALMERS.
THE STATE IN ITS RELATION TO EDUCATION. By Sir HENRY CRAIK, K.C.B.

THE ENGLISH CONSTITUTION. By EMILE BOUTMY. Translated from the French by ISABEL M. EADEN. With Introduction by Sir FREDERICK POLLOCK, Bart. Crown 8vo, 6s.
STUDIES IN CONSTITUTIONAL LAW—FRANCE, ENGLAND, UNITED STATES. Translated from the Second French Edition by E. M. DICEY. With an Introduction by A. V. DICEY, B.C.L. Crown 8vo, 6s.
SPEECHES ON QUESTIONS OF PUBLIC POLICY. By RICHARD COBDEN, M.P. Edited by JOHN BRIGHT and JAMES E. THOROLD ROGERS. Globe 8vo, 3s. 6d.
INTRODUCTION TO THE STUDY OF POLITICAL ECONOMY. By LUIGI COSSA, Professor in the Royal University of Pavia. Revised by the Author and translated from the Italian by LOUIS DYER, M.A. Crown 8vo, 8s. 6d. net.
INTRODUCTION TO THE STUDY OF THE LAW OF THE CONSTITUTION. By A. V. DICEY, B.C.L. Fifth Edition. 8vo, 12s. 6d.
THE ENGLISH CONSTITUTION. A Commentary on its Nature and Growth. By JESSE MACY, M.A., Professor of Political Science in Iowa College. Extra crown 8vo, 8s. 6d. net.
THE LAWS AND JURISPRUDENCE OF ENGLAND AND AMERICA. Being a Series of Lectures delivered before Yale University. By JOHN F. DILLON, LL.D. 8vo, 16s. net.
THE GOVERNMENT OF VICTORIA (AUSTRALIA). By EDWARD JENKS, M.A. 8vo, 14s.
LECTURES ON THE GROWTH OF CRIMINAL LAW IN ANCIENT COMMUNITIES. By RICHARD R. CHERRY, LL.D. 8vo, 5s. net.

MACMILLAN AND CO., LTD., LONDON.

www.ingramcontent.com/pod-product-compliance
Lightning Source LLC
Chambersburg PA
CBHW030608270326
41927CB00007B/1095